INSIGHT GUIDES

GREAT BREAKS
DEVON & CORNWALL

PLAN & BOOK
YOUR TAILOR-MADE TRIP

BRAZIL **CHILE** **ECUADOR**

TAILOR-MADE TRIPS & UNIQUE EXPERIENCES CREATED BY LOCAL TRAVEL EXPERTS AT INSIGHTGUIDES.COM/HOLIDAYS

Insight Guides has been inspiring travellers with high-quality travel content for over 45 years. As well as our popular guidebooks, we now offer the opportunity to book tailor-made private trips completely personalised to your needs and interests. By connecting with one of our local experts, you will directly benefit from their expertise and local know-how, helping you create memories that will last a lifetime.

HOW INSIGHTGUIDES.COM/HOLIDAYS WORKS

STEP 1

Pick your dream destination and submit an enquiry, or modify an existing itinerary if you prefer.

STEP 2

Fill in a short form, sharing details of your travel plans and preferences with a local expert.

STEP 3

Your local expert will create your personalised itinerary, which you can amend until you are completely satisfied.

STEP 4

Book securely online. Pack your bags and enjoy your holiday! Your local expert will be available to answer questions during your trip.

BENEFITS OF PLANNING & BOOKING AT INSIGHTGUIDES.COM/HOLIDAYS

PLANNED BY LOCAL EXPERTS
The Insight Guides local experts are hand-picked, based on their experience in the travel industry and their impeccable standards of customer service.

SAVE TIME & MONEY
When a local expert plans your trip, you save time and money when you book, even during high season. You won't be charged for using a credit card either.

TAILOR-MADE TRIPS
Book with Insight Guides, and you will be in complete control of the planning process, from the initial selections to amending your final itinerary.

BOOK & TRAVEL STRESS-FREE
Enjoy stress-free travel when you use the Insight Guides secure online booking platform. All bookings come with a money-back guarantee.

WHAT OTHER TRAVELLERS THINK ABOUT TRIPS BOOKED AT INSIGHTGUIDES.COM/HOLIDAYS

Trip to Portugal

Every step of the planning process and the trip itself was effortless and exceptional. Our special interests, preferences and requests were accommodated resulting in a trip that exceeded our expectations.

Corinne, USA ★★★★★

Trip to Vietnam

The organization was superb, the drivers professional, and accommodation quite comfortable. I was well taken care of! My thanks to your colleagues who helped make my trip to Vietnam such a great experience.

Heather ★★★★★

Contents

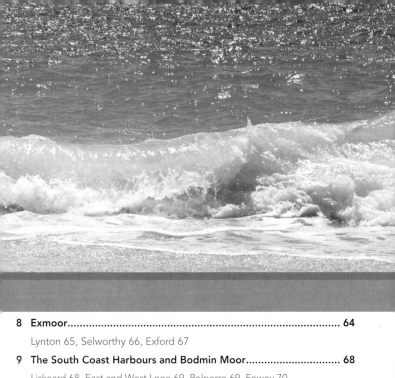

Devon & Cornwall's Top 10

Many miles of wonderful coastal scenery, spectacular beaches, wild moorlands and great gardens make this the place to be outdoors. Indoors, you can see the art and architecture the landscape has inspired.

▲ **Dartmoor** ranges from moorland to steep wooded valleys and secluded villages. See page 46.

▲ **Lynmouth Cliff Railway.** Designed by a student of Brunel, it links Lynmouth with Lynton. See page 66.

▲ **Dartmouth.** This is where the Britannia Royal Naval College trains officers. See page 33.

▶ **Tate St Ives.** A sister of the London galleries, which has long been a magnet for artists. See page 96.

▲ **Surfing.** Fistral Bay near Newquay – the best surf beaches in Britain are along Cornwall's north coast. See page 100.

▲ **Torquay.** Queen of the English Riviera, Torquay is an elegant resort where Edwardian and modern architecture blends. See page 24.

▲ **Tresco Abbey Gardens.** Vibrant gardens flourish in the mild climate of the Scilly Isles. See page 110.

▼ **Tintagel.** Feel the power of myths at King Arthur's legendary Cornish castle. See page 104.

▼ **Eden Project.** Cornwall's most popular attraction. See page 78.

▼ **Exeter.** Devon's county capital, Exeter has a majestic 14th-century cathedral. See page 14.

A typical Cornish rural scene.

Overview

A West Country Welcome

Warm, sometimes wet, always wonderful, this peninsula of high cliffs and moors, cream teas and thatched cottages has some of the most spectacular scenery in Britain.

Devon and Cornwall are beloved British holiday destinations. Beautiful, dramatic seascapes of high cliffs, delightful coves and broad, sandy beaches sweep along the extensive coastlines north and south. Fishing villages sit snug in coves, and river estuaries sigh with the ebb and flow of the gathering Atlantic tide. Small wonder artists have been drawn here.

If Cornwall inspires painters, Devon, the county that *Country Life* magazine once declared the best in Britain in which to live, attracts writers. 'Deepest Devon' is an environmentally aware, agricultural land of thatched cottages and cream teas, run through with dancing river valleys and blind, winding lanes.

LEGEND AND REALITY

Covering 1,376 sq miles (3,563 sq km), Cornwall is a little over half the size of Devon. But this is the land of King Arthur, big on legend and fantasy, with pixies, smugglers, pirates, wreckers and saints, underpinned by haunting relics of mysterious and ancient cultures. On misty moorland and along its rocky coast, prehistoric stone circles and burial chambers, cliff castles and hill forts punctuate the landscape, along with gaunt ruins from disused mines. Tin has been found and traded here since Phoenician times.

CLIMATE

Mild and sunny, warmed by the prevailing southwesterly wind – which also brings rain – the region is hospitable all year round. Flowers flourish everywhere; hedgerows are nature's gardens, while Devon violets and Cornish daffodils are among the first seasonal blooms in the shops each year. Spring comes early to the far west, and autumn lingers until late into the year.

When moisture-laden Atlantic winds hit the coast and swirl up to the exposed moors, they let go their load. Dartmoor, at 2,037ft (600m) the highest part of southern England, and Exmoor not far behind, each re-

A clifftop wild-flower carpet.

Bronze statue honouring Cornish fishermen lost at sea, on the waterfront in Newlyn, Cornwall.

ceives up to 90ins (230cm) of rain a year. Rivers can swell and burst their banks with disastrous results.

But this is also the location of the 'English Riviera', in South Devon. The balmy, sheltered, palm-tree-lined resorts of Torbay hold the record for the warmest and sunniest days in Britain, with average September temperatures of 17.5°C (63.5°F).

The north coast is more inhospitable, and it shares with Cornwall a reputation for being a ships' graveyard. But that means good surfing too – some of Britain's best surf beaches are to be found here.

SEAGOING HERITAGE

The South Devon coast has a variety of safe anchorages, creeks and estuaries that in their day attracted traders and ship-builders. Crusaders and *Mayflower* pilgrims set off from these southern shores. Devon was the birthplace of the Elizabethan buccaneers Francis Drake and Sir Walter Raleigh, and many Devonians have travelled widely in the merchant navy or in the armed forces, both of which have bases in the county, at Plymouth and Dartmouth.

Cornwall's maritime past is vital to its identity. Along 300 miles (482km) of varied coastline the spirit of 'free traders' is enshrined in the names of hidden coves, secret tunnels and caverns, and in the history of wonderful old inns. Cornwall's fishing activity fascinates the visitor at busy harbours such as Newlyn, Mevagissey and Looe, and the county's noble tradition of lifesaving is enshrined in lifeboat houses and coastguard lookouts.

ECONOMY AND TOURISM

Tourism is vital to the economies of these two counties, where natural resources are scant, and major commercial centres a long way away. Businesses tend to be small and self-employment is high.

Wage levels as a whole are among the UK's lowest. Traditional industries such as agriculture, forestry and fishing are low down on the list of money-making activities. However after the economic recession and several poor summers, visitor numbers saw substantial growth for the region, peaking with the heatwave of 2018.

Devon alone numbers some 100,000 self-employed people, while receiving more than six million visitors annually. The county, along with neighbouring Cornwall, is turning increasingly to new enterprises, such as further enhancing the production of locally sourced food and drink and employing green energy solutions. Initiatives are supported by the South West Tourism Alliance (www.swtourismalliance.org.uk).

Cornwall's remoteness meanwhile creates economic difficulties. The old Cornish industries have long been in decline; tin and copper mining are no longer viable, despite a conviction that Cornwall still holds vast mineral wealth in deep deposits. Of the old extractive industries, only a limited form of china clay and quarrying survive.

Cornwall's other great traditional industry, fishing, is struggling, and many must progressively rely on tourism. More than five million visitors arrive annually, generating a quarter of the county's GDP and employing one in five of the local population.

WARM HOSPITALITY

Independence is at the heart of the local character. According to surveys, a West Country accent is one of the most desirable in Britain. Cornwall, once with its own language – at present undergoing a revival – retains a rebellious streak. But you will find the friendliest of hosts, and people who still have time to stop and chat. Don't be surprised if they call you 'my lover' or 'my handsome'. And if a Cornish person says *dynargh*, they are only offering you a 'welcome'.

Guide to Coloured Boxes

Eating	This guide is dotted
Fact	with coloured boxes providing additional
Green	practical and cultural information to
Kids	make the most of
Shopping	your visit. Here is a guide to the coding
View	system.

The revitalised quayside in Exeter, Devon.

Food and Drink

Shimmeringly fresh fish, lovingly matured farmhouse cheeses, crusty cottage loaves, local ales, award-winning wines, organic apple juice and traditional ice cream are just some of the delicious food and drink in Devon and Cornwall. Added to that is the shift in cooking trends and tastes, led by Padstow chef Rick Stein and household favourite Jamie Oliver, who have been making West Country eateries fashionable. But good food is to be found everywhere, as inns offer meals that go far beyond basic pub grub. Sustainability is key, and local means just that.

DELICIOUS DEVON

The food industry has a long tradition in Devon, dating back to the days when the ports were in their prime and flotillas needed provisioning. This tradition, combined with a scattered local population, has kept the supermarket culture at bay, with the result that Devon is now one of a decreasing number of regions where small town centres still have thriving markets, shops and traditional grocers.

Cornish pasties, devised as an all-in-one lunch for workers.

The huge Devonshire cream tea business is serviced by a large number of local dairies, which also produce a wide variety of local cheeses. This includes the Ticklemore Cheese dairy near Totnes, which specialises in blue cheese and supplies local shops including Country Cheeses in Tavistock. Another speciality is ice cream; try Salcome Dairy products in local shops; Dunstaple Farm supplies the Exmoor area, and the Dartmouth Ice Cream Company, with its shop, The Good Intent, located in the town.

The fishing industry is still important in the south of the county, so menus are strong on seafood. Local specialities to look out for are Brixham plaice, Dartmouth dressed crab and Salcombe smokies (smoked mackerel). There's a strong trade in home-made produce at most markets, with quality baking, as well as chutneys, mustards, marmalades and preserves of every kind on offer. One of the best locations is the Barnstaple pannier market (Mon–Sat 9am–4pm) alongside the Butcher's Row line of shops.

Devonian drinking

Cider apples grow everywhere, and some rural pubs serve local scrumpy, drawn from a barrel under the bar. Scrumpy can be an acquired taste, and packs a considerable punch. Grapes grow well in the south, with vineyards at Bickleigh (near Tiverton), Lower Eastcott (near Okehampton), and in a lovely location down to the shores of the Dart at Sharpham (Ashprington, near Totnes). Devon breweries include the well-established Dartmoor Brewery and Exmoor Ales, while small craft beer producers are on the increase,

Food Festivals

Celebrate all things foodie at these festivals. For more information, visit www.visitdevon.co.uk and www.visitcornwall.com.

May: Exeter Festival of South West England Food and Drink; Axminster River Cottage Food Fair; St Ives Food and Drink Festival; Salcombe Crab Fest.

June: Plymouth Flavour Fest; Crediton Food Festival.

August: Newlyn Fish Festival.

September: Newquay Fish Festival; Abbfest Food and Drink Festival, Newton Abbot.

October: Falmouth Oyster Festival; Dartmouth Food Festival.

Devon's acclaimed dairy farms mean superior cream teas.

such as the Powderkeg Brewery in Woodbury Salterton, near Exeter.

CORNISH CUISINE

Cornwall has many traditional foods, but the Cornish pasty has become symbol as much as sustenance. Essentially an early form of 'fast food', the pasty evolved as an all-in-one lunch for miners, fishermen and farmers. A real Cornish pasty is a crescent-shaped pie of shortcrust pastry, crimped along one side. The traditional filling is chuck steak, chopped turnip, potatoes and onion, seasoned with salt and pepper.

It's a short step from pasties to pies, and here the Cornish cook is resourceful. Squab pie is filled, not with young pigeons as the name suggests, but with a mixture of lamb, apple, onions and sometimes prunes. Another favourite is Stargazy pie, made traditionally with pilchards.

The most traditional Cornish food is to be found in the seafood restaurants. You can expect salmon from the Tamar and the Camel on menus in those areas, and farmed trout almost everywhere. But best in the west of the county are lobster and crab, served in a variety of ways, together with oysters from Helford River and Newlyn crab chowder.

Cakes and ale

Figgy pudding is baked with suet, flour, eggs, sugar and raisins (not figs). Lighter alternatives are saffron buns, saffron cake and Cornish splits, cut in half and filled with clotted cream and jam. Cornish Yarg cheese, wrapped in nettles, has gained in popularity. And don't miss Metheglin (mead) and the local Spingo and Sharp's beers.

For more culinary information, visit: www.eatoutdevon.com, www.eatoutcornwall.com and www.tasteofthewest.co.uk.

Find our recommended restaurants at the end of each Tour. Below is a Price Guide to help you make your choice.

Eating Out Price Guide

Two-course meal for one person, including a glass of wine.
£££ = over £30
££ = £20–30
£ = under £20

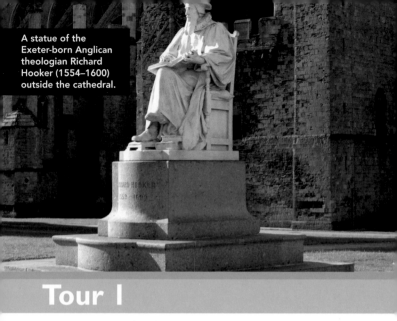

A statue of the Exeter-born Anglican theologian Richard Hooker (1554–1600) outside the cathedral.

Exeter and Topsham

Explore the highlights of this historic cathedral city and port on a full-day, 6-mile (9km) walking tour.

The county capital, **Exeter** lies on the River Exe in South Devon not far from the sea. It's a grand old market town (pop. 1224,200) enlivened by one of Britain's oldest universities and an international airport.

The first recorded settlement (85–80BC) here was named Isca Dumnoniorum, after the local Dumnoniorum tribe. Around 100 years later the Romans transferred their West Country base from Seaton to Exeter, and the city began to take shape. In medieval times it prospered through farming and the wool trade, and it hallmarked its own silver until the early 19th century. But as ships grew larger, the river's facilities became inadequate, and it lost out to larger ports. Today it is seen as one of the top places to do business in Britain.

Highlights

- Cathedral
- Underground Passages
- Royal Albert Memorial Museum
- Quayside
- Topsham

AROUND THE CATHEDRAL

The focal point for any visitor is the elegant **Cathedral Close**, screened from the modern city by a facade of buildings with a spread of diverse styles from several centuries.

At its centre stands the handsome **Cathedral Church of St Peter ❶** (the Close; tel: 01392-285 983; www. exeter-cathedral.org.uk; Mon–Sat 9am–5pm, Sun 11.30am–5pm; restric-

Pick your own, go fishing or pat a pig at Darts Farm.

Fun on the Farm

For family fun head on down to Darts Farm in Topsham (tel: 01392-878 200; www.dartsfarm.co.uk). Pick up a map at the farm shop, then find your way through the maize maze (summer only). There are walks round the farm and an animal corner where you can meet the resident pigs, sheep, cows and chickens. Older kids can try fishing on the ponds for carp, bream and roach before picking their own fruit to take home.

tions during services). Largely 14th century, its two towers date from 1050, when Bishop Leofric established a see here. He was enthroned on the site, with King Edward the Confessor in attendance. The nave is of Beer stone, started by Bishop Bronescombe (1257–80) and completed by Bishop Grandisson (1327–69).

The visitor entrance is located in the **West Front**, which is animated by figures of apostles and prophets, at ground level much weathered by devotional fingers. Inside, the most significant feature is the **fan vaulting**, which extends in a web of stone for 300ft (90m), the longest Gothic vault in the world. Outside the West Front is where most of Exeter Council's free Red Coat Guided Tours meet (tel: 01392-265 203; www.exeter.gov.uk/guidedtours).

The most eye-catching building in the close is the timber-framed 16th-century **Mol's Coffee House** ❷ (now a high-end shop) where Sir Francis Drake supposedly met his captains. Diagonally across, **The Royal Clarence**, founded in 1769, claims the title of Britain's first hotel – although it was actually just the first to be called a hotel, thanks to its French owner. Unfortunately, the hotel was destroyed by fire in 2016 and is currently being rebuilt (completion date unclear at the time of writing).

Tacked onto the corner next to Mol's is the small sandstone **St Martin's Church** ❸ (founded 1065), which has a slightly crooked interior. Up St Martin's Lane to the left is the Ship Inn, also a Drake hangout.

MODERN CITY

St Martin's Lane emerges onto the largely pedestrianised High Street. The post-war rebuilding of Exeter is clearly visible here: to the northeast the street widens into a view of stolid modern buildings, while to the southwest it narrows into the uneven styles of old Exeter, with some medieval wood-timbered frontages.

Beneath the pavements of the modern area are the **Underground Passages** ❹ (Paris Street, entrance in arcaded Roman Gate Passage; tel: 01392-665 887; June–Sept Mon–Sat 9.30am–5.30pm, Sun 10.30am–4pm, May–Oct Tue–Fri 10.30am–4.30pm, Sat 9.30am–5.30pm, Sun 11.30am–4pm), 14th-century tunnels that were carved out of the rock on the initiative of the clergy to help distribute water from a distant spring through the growing city. Although there is not much to see, the underground guided tours are entertaining and the experience unique, if cramped.

Up the hill behind the passages is **Exeter Castle** ❺ (also known as Rougemont Castle). Not a lot remains of the castle, and many of the buildings are now luxury apartments and used for events, but you can visit the courtyard, and the gardens are a delightful spot.

SHOPS, ART AND HISTORY

Retracing your steps to St Martin's Lane, diagonally to the north is the narrow **Gandy Street**, with murals and speciality shops. Topping a rise on the right is **Exeter Phoenix** ❻ (01392-667 080; www.exeterphoenix.org.uk) an arts and

media centre with a popular café-bar and a packed schedule of events.

Straight ahead you'll find the **Royal Albert Memorial Museum (RAMM)** ❼ (Queen Street; tel: 01392-265 858; www.rammuseum. org.uk; Tue–Sun 10am–5pm; free), which features an eclectic mix from pre-history to fine art and world culture. Housed in a beautiful Victorian building, the award-winning museum's 16 modern galleries are well-presented with lots of interactive displays that enhance the visitor's experience. Back on the High Street further down, on the right-hand side heading south, is the tottery-looking Tudor portico of the **Guildhall** ❽ (tel: 01392-665 500; times vary so check; free). It is the oldest functioning guildhall in the country: there has been a hall here from 1160, although the present building dates from the 14th century.

As it descends towards the river, High Street turns into Fore Street. Up narrow Mint Lane on the right is **St Nicholas Priory** ❾, the guest wing of a former priory, now brightly painted and furnished in the style of 1602, when it belonged to the Hurst family.

Back to Fore Street, descend the hill the other side of it and you will eventually reach the river Exe and the cobbled **Quayside** ❿ where history, antiques markets, craft workshops and nightlife live side by side. The visitor centre (tel: 01392-271 611; Apr–Oct daily 10am–5pm, Nov–Mar Sat–

The tidal estuary at Topsham is a rich habitat for waterfowl.

Sun 11am–4pm; free) gives a taste of what Exeter's port was like in its heyday and is located in the old **Customs House ⑪**, built in 1680.

TOPSHAM

Continue walking or cycle 4 miles (6km) along the canal to **Topsham ⑫**, the estuary port at the mouth of the canal southeast of Exeter. During the height of the woollen trade in the 17th century, when the Exeter quayside began to prove inadequate, the merchants started to build grand houses on the shore at Topsham, creating an elegant waterside where passenger steamers used to dock until the railways came. The boatyards are still active.

Topsham's narrow-street charm is considerable. Antique shops, old inns and restaurants line the main street, and along the Strand many of the houses are

Inside the café-bar of Exeter Phoenix.

gable-ended, in imitation of Dutch style, a fashion introduced by Topsham merchants returning from Holland. Among them is the Shell House (1718), named after the lovely scallop shell in its doorway.

All the houses have fine views over the Exe estuary, which is a rich habitat for waterfowl.

Eating Out

Exeter
The Fat Pig
2 John Street; tel: 01392-437 217; www.fatpig-exeter.co.uk; food served Mon–Fri 5–10pm, Sat noon–10pm, Sun noon–5pm.
The team at this convivial pub serve buzzy British dishes, smoke their own ham and bake their own bread. ££
The Oddfellows
60 New North Road; tel: 01392-209 050; www.theoddfellowsbar.co.uk; food served Tue–Thu 5.30–9pm, Fri & Sat until 10pm.
Relaxed, friendly gastro bar and cocktail lounge with a modern English menu featuring local produce lovingly prepared. ££
On the Waterfront
4–9 The Quay; tel: 01392-210 590; www.waterfrontexeter.co.uk; daily lunch and dinner.
Perched on the edge of the water

in a 19th-century warehouse, this restaurant/pub serves tasty tapas, pizzas, fresh fish, meats, pastas and salads. £
Topsham
The Fish Shed
Darts Farm Village; tel: 01392-878 206; www.dartsfarm.co.uk; Tue–Sat 11.30am–7.30pm, Sun 9am–3.30pm.
Select your fresh line-caught fish straight from the slab and a fisherman chef will grill it in olive oil or fry it in beer batter. £
The Galley Fish & Seafood Restaurant
41 Fore Street; tel: 01392-876 078; www.galleyrestaurant.co.uk; Tue–Sat lunch and dinner.
With stunning views over the estuary, this popular restaurant serves prime fresh fish and local produce, delivered in creative and subtle dishes. ££

Branscombe's picturesque church.

Tour 2

East Devon

This is farming country, dotted with market towns and edged with elegant seaside resorts, which can all be taken in on a 50-mile (80km) full-day car tour.

This tour starts at the town of **Exmouth ❶**, where the River Exe meets the sea. Its 2 miles (3km) of golden sand are the finest in East Devon. As one of the first seaside holiday spots, the Exmouth seafront has all the traditional attractions of a resort, as well as a big windsurfing centre.

Two miles (3km) out of Exmouth just off the Exeter road, **A La Ronde ❷** (NT; tel: 01395-265 514; daily Feb–Oct 11am–5pm) sits high on the hill with amazing views over the estuary. This eccentric 16-sided house was designed in 1795 by Jane Parminter, who, helped by her cousin Mary, decorated it with feathers and seashells, seaweed and sand, cut paper and marbled paint.

Highlights

- Exmouth
- A La Ronde
- Otterton Mill
- Bicton Park
- Branscombe
- Beer Quarry Caves

Leaving Exmouth, the B3178 winds around the hills before descending into **Budleigh Salterton**, a genteel place, with a long shingle beach framed in a red-cliff bay. At the east end are salt flats where the River Otter reaches the sea. Sir Walter Raleigh was born a couple of miles away at East Budleigh.

Windsurfing at Exmouth.

OTTERTON MILL

Two miles (3km) inland, towards Bicton, is a crossroads with a brick signpost that dates from 1743. Here in this lovely valley is **Otterton**, a village of attractive whitewashed cob houses with a stream beside the main street heading for the River Otter. In 1414 there were two woollen mills and a flour mill in the village, and boats could anchor by the bridge. **Otterton Mill ❸** (tel: 01395-568 521; www.ottertonmill.com; daily Apr–Oct 10am–5pm, Nov–Mar 10am–4pm; free) is still functioning, in a complex with a restaurant, art and crafts centre, and shops selling local produce.

A couple of miles up the road is **Bicton Park and House ❹** (tel:

01395-568 465; www.bictongardens.co.uk; daily Apr–Sept 10am–5pm, Oct–Mar 10am–4.30pm). Henry Rolle's country house garden design of 1730 has been embellished with palm house, museum and a railway.

A right turn on the A3052 will bring you down into the crowded valley of **Sidmouth ❺**, the most attractive and best preserved of East Devon's resorts. Narrow lanes of tearooms and traditional shops back onto a grand seafront dominated by a parade of Regency houses with wrought-iron balconies.

Take the A3052 east for a couple of miles to the **Donkey Sanctuary** (www.thedonkeysanctuary.org.uk; daily 9am–5pm, Nov–Feb until 4pm), a rest home for mistreated donkeys.

BRANSCOMBE AND BEER

From the sanctuary, a lane descends into the village of **Branscombe ❻** (meaning branched combe or valley). There are corners of real beauty and character here; at the top end of the village is the 12th-century Norman church dedicated to the Welsh saint, Winifred. Grapes used to be grown in this sheltered valley for the monks of Sherborne Abbey.

The Jurassic Coast

Keen walkers can follow the South West Coast Path from Exmouth to Beer Head. This is part of the Jurassic Coast natural World Heritage Site, which continues to Studland Bay in Dorset, representing 185 million years of Earth history in 95 miles (153km) of coast. The East Devon rusty red section is the oldest and is home to Britain's richest mid-Triassic reptile sites. More info: www.jurassiccoast.org; www. southwestcoastpath.org.uk.

The Jurassic Coast has some of the richest fossil finds in the world.

Branscombe was also known for its lace-makers, as was the next-door village of **Beer** (derived from 'beare', meaning wood), up over the hill. But besides smuggling and lace, Beer's fame comes from its limestone, used to build Exeter Cathedral and many other great churches and country houses of the region. Beer stone is unusual in that it is relatively soft and easy to quarry but hardens on exposure to air. Part of the former underground workings are open to the public, on the Branscombe to Beer road, in **Beer Quarry Caves** ❼ (tel: 01297-680 282; www.beerquarry caves.co.uk; daily April–Sept at 10am,

The shingle and pebble beach at Branscombe.

tours every hour on the half hour from 10.30am, last tour 3.30pm, Oct reduced times). In these vaulted caverns, which supplied stone for 24 cathedrals, everything was done by hand. Many of the masons carved their names on the walls, and the pick marks made by the Romans are still visible.

Up the hill above Beer, **Pecorama** (tel: 01297-21542; www.pecorama. info; indoor exhibition all year, outdoor attractions daily Apr–Oct 10am– 5.30pm; reduced facilities and times Nov–Mar) is an excellent diversion for children, with rides on small trains, entertainers, an outdoor play area and crazy golf.

The village of Beer itself clusters around a short main street which ends with a brief drop to the beach, where fishing boats are winched up and down the shingle. Beer's buccaneering past is still remembered in an annual regatta.

It is difficult to tell where Beer ends and **Seaton** begins, but the two places are very different. Seaton is a big, holiday-camp-based resort spread across the flat of the Axe valley, with a good beach and little of further interest other than the **Electric Tramway** (www. tram.co.uk), which runs up-valley in summer to the small town of Colyton.

Shute Barton, a battlemented medieval manor house dating from the 14th century, and one of the most important examples of its kind.

On the side of the Shute road out of Colyton stands the imposing gateway of **Shute Barton** (started in 1380). Administered by the National Trust and primarily a holiday cottage, the house is open to the public for tours four times a year (see National Trust website, www. nationaltrust.org.uk, for times).

HONITON

Continue on the A35 to the market town of **Honiton** ❽, administrative capital of East Devon. In the mid-19th century there were more than 4,000 makers of Honiton lace in the area, but the industry has since died. Presentation pieces are still made privately and have been worn by all the recent royal babies. Examples are kept in All Hallows Museum (www.honitonmuseum.co.uk; mid-Mar–Oct Mon–Fri 9.30am–3.30pm, Sat until 12.30pm) in the town centre and the Honiton Lace Shop (see box).

A third of the way back to Exeter, south of the A30, is **Ottery St Mary**, a particularly attractive, largely 17th- and 18th-century town (Otrei in the Domesday Book) wedged into a small valley. The romantic poet Samuel Taylor Coleridge, son of the local vicar, was born here in 1772. Up a steep hill from the centre is **St Mary** ❾, a stunning

Shops around Honiton

Many Honiton women still make lace as a hobby. Buy a sample or try out a lacemaking kit at the Honiton Lace Shop, The Barn, Elmfield Farm, Weston nr Honiton (by appointment only; tel: 01404-42416; www. honitonlace.com), or buy online. On Corrymoor farm in Stockland, Honiton (tel: 01404-861 245; www.corrymoor. com), the Whiteley family raises pedigree angora goats for mohair socks. The Brook Gallery, Fore Street, Budleigh Salterton (tel: 01395-443 003; www.brookgallery.co.uk) is the place to buy original prints and etchings.

Floral designs are typical of Honiton's bobbin lace.

The beautiful fan vaulting in St Mary's church, Ottery St Mary, echoes that of Exeter Cathedral.

replica of Exeter Cathedral, far more impressive from the inside than out. The church was founded by Bishop Grandisson, who completed Exeter Cathedral, and has a matching 14th-century astronomical clock.

A mile or so northwest of Ottery, and visible from the B3174, is **Cadhay** ❿ (tel: 01404-813 511; www.cadhay.org. uk; May–Sept Fri 2–5.30pm, also late May and August public holidays), a private house built around 1550 by solicitor John Haydon, probably using stone from local churches demolished by Henry VIII; every room has a different character. The house and its cottages are available for self-catering holidays. From Cadhay it is a mile (1.5km) to the A30, and thence back to Exeter.

Eating Out

Exmouth
Brasserie 16
16 Douglas Avenue; tel: 01395-270 222; www.brasserie16.co.uk; daily breakfast, Wed, Fri & Sun lunch and Wed–Sun dinner.
The restaurant of the Devoncourt Hotel is set in fabulous subtropical gardens near Lyme Bay. At lunch-time on Wednesdays, Fridays and Sundays there is a renowned carvery. ££
Les Saveurs
9 Tower Street; tel: 01395-269 459; www.saveursrestaurant.com; Tue dinner only, Wed–Sat lunch and dinner.
For lovers of fresh seafood and fish, this is a must, and there are choices for carnivores, too. All are cooked with French flair, using seasonal, fresh Devon produce. £££

Beer
Steamers
New Cut; tel: 01297-22922; www. steamersrestaurant.co.uk; Tue–Sat 10am–1.45pm, 6.45–9pm.

Excellent for locally-sourced produce from roast lamb shank to sautéed scallops, Steamers is particularly popular for its seafood and fresh fish dishes. ££

Otterton
Otterton Mill
Otterton Mill; tel: 01395-567 041; www.ottertonmill.com; daily 10am–5pm (check website Nov–Mar).
Dine on freshly cooked specials and interesting platters either inside this historic mill building or outside on the sun terrace. This is also a good place for breakfast or a cream tea. £

Honiton
Toast
155 High Street; tel: 01404-598 067; Mon–Sat 8.30am–5pm, Sun 9.30am–4pm.
A little haven in the heart of Honiton, this café and pâtisserie does full English breakfast, tasty sandwiches, daily specials and delicious high tea with home-made scones. There is also a garden for those sunny days. £

Powderham Castle, home of the 18th Earl of Devon.

Tour 3

The English Riviera

This 49-mile (79km) half-day tour explores this coast, defined by sunny promenades, broad beaches and a refined gentility.

From Dawlish to the River Dart, Devon dedicates itself to tourism. Sheltered from the prevailing winds, this coast is a few degrees warmer all year round, making balmy resorts out of pretty fishing villages. The main attraction here is Torbay, not a town but an administrative umbrella for Torquay, Paignton and Brixham within 22 miles (35km) of the great sweep of Tor Bay.

POWDERHAM CASTLE

A short drive southeast from Exeter, in stunning parkland overlooking the estuary, is **Powderham Castle ❶** (tel: 01636-890 243; www.powderham.co.uk; Apr–Oct Sun–Fri 11am–4.30pm), fiefdom of the Courtenay family, earls of Devon, and featured in the film *The Remains of the Day*. The

Highlights

- Powderham Castle
- Torquay Seafront
- Brixham
- Kent's Cavern
- Dartmouth Steam Railway and River Boat Company
- Paignton Zoo

building dates from 1390, the interior is grand and dramatic, and the guided tours are entertaining. Take the tractor trailer ride for a deer park safari.

Powderham's main entrance faced the estuary, until Isambard Kingdom Brunel bought the foreshore from the Courtenays and the Crown and built his railway. Today the line is a feature of this shore for many miles, such as at

Wedding day at Babbacombe Model Village – England in miniature.

Dawlish. Dawlish first became popular towards the end of the 18th century, and both Charles Dickens and Jane Austen stayed here. It made the headlines in February 2014 when part of the sea wall was breached, flooding the railway line, which remained closed for two months. Wilder bird life can be found on **Dawlish Warren**, the sandbar that covers most of the entrance to the Exe estuary. The sand-dune-backed Blue Flag beach is a popular picnic site.

Teignmouth, further down the A379, has a split personality. To the open sea it presents itself as a resort, with Grand Pier (1860s) and long beach, while the other side of the town lies along the Teign estuary and is still a working port. The coast road crosses the estuary via a former toll bridge

to reach the pretty village of **Shaldon**, and then climbs the hill behind it, affording good views of the estuary.

TORBAY

You are now entering the Torbay area, although this approach is uninspiring and it is not until the **seafront** that **Torquay's ❷** full glory is revealed. The town is formed around inner and outer harbours filled with leisure boats and swanky yachts, a pier and spacious esplanade. The main shopping street, tunnels back up the valley. Undergoing a style revival, the harbourside and promenade has cafés, boat trips and the **Pavilion theatre**, a lovely example of Edwardian wedding-cake seaside architecture but now empty – redevelopment proposals have left its future uncertain. Torquay emphasises its Mediterranean influences, and

The Riviera Line

One of the most scenic stretches of railway, the line from Exeter to Paignton sweeps along the sea wall and offers spectacular views of the Exe estuary and the red cliffs of the English Channel coastline. Much of the surrounding countryside is a designated wildlife reserve. The line, built by Brunel in the 1840s, runs alongside the sea to Teignmouth before turning inland to Newton Abbot. From there it climbs and descends into Paignton.

For 28 miles (45km), the railway sweeps along the coast.

at night, with its illuminations and rustling palm trees, it could be Cannes (almost), and is also gaining a reputation as a foodie destination.

Several attractions are concentrated around the former village of **Babbacombe**, on the north side of the Torquay promontory. The focus is the manicured lawns on top of an east-facing cliff overlooked by elegant small hotels, with Oddicombe beach way down below. The beach is reached by a zigzagging road, or by the **Babbacombe Cliff Railway ③** (tel: 01803-328 750; www.babbacombecliffrailway.co.uk; mid-Feb–Oct daily; also weekends Nov–Dec), an attraction in itself. A short walk inland from the cliffs is the **Babbacombe Model Village ④** (tel: 01803-315 315; www.babbacombe modelvillage.co.uk; daily 10am–last entry 4pm, with exceptions), contemporary England in microcosm, with sound and movement, created with much care and humour – look for the Ann Teak furniture shop and Annie Seedballs, the confectioners.

BYGONES AND KENT'S CAVERN

A short walk away, in Fore Street, is **Bygones ⑤** (tel: 01803-326 108; www.bygones.co.uk; daily Apr–Oct 10am–

The promenade at Torquay, the Riviera's main resort, can have a dazzling Mediterranean air.

5pm, Nov–Mar 10am–4pm), an indoor fantasyland of sights, sounds and smells, with a Victorian shopping street, model railways and a rather odd World War I trench experience.

Travelling a couple of miles southeast along the same road, **Kent's Cavern ⑥** (tel: 01803-215 136; www.kents-cavern.co.uk; daily 9am–5pm, guided tour only) is a network of limestone caves created two million years ago by underground rivers.

More than 80,000 archaeological artefacts have been found here, the best of them housed in **Torquay Museum ⑦** (www.torquaymuseum.org; Mon–Sat 10am–4pm) on Babbacombe Road. Rated one of the best museums in Southwest England, the displays include artefacts from Kent's Cavern, a reconstruction of a Devon farmhouse and a

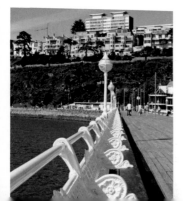

gallery dedicated to one-time Torquay resident, thriller-writer Agatha Christie.

On the other side of the harbour, away from the seafront, is **Torre Abbey** ❽ (www.torre-abbey.org.uk; tel: 01803-293 593; Tue–Sun 10am–5pm, also some public holidays). Torbay's art collection is housed in this 122-room former Abbey, once the largest of its kind in Britain, and visitors can see what it was like to live as a 12th-century Augustinian monk. Agatha Christie used to visit when the Abbey was a private home, and you can detect plants used for murderous poisons in the restored medieval garden.

Beyond Torre lies **Cockington**, a preserved rural village and country house in extensive grounds.

PAIGNTON

In the centre of Tor Bay, Torquay blends seamlessly into tacky **Paignton** ❾. Abundant with arcades and fast-food outlets, it does good business serving as it does two of the region's best stretches of sand, one off the promenade in front of the town centre, the other at Goodrington, a little further on.

Goodrington can be reached via the **Dartmouth Steam Railway and River Boat Company** ❿ (tel: 01803-555 872; www.dartmouthrail river.co.uk; Apr–Oct daily, limited time-table rest of year), which sets off from Paignton and chugs through attractive coastal scenery to its terminus at King-swear (see page 33), on the Dart estuary, where boat tours are available.

Up the valley behind Goodrington is **Paignton Zoo** ⓫ (tel: 01803-697 500; www.paigntonzoo.org.uk; summer daily 10am–6pm, winter closing times vary so check on the website), well landscaped and innovative, and home to more than 2,500 animals living in natural habitats. Micro-environments re-created here include tropical forest, savannah and wetlands.

Beyond Paignton, the bay becomes less populated, and the road winds through countryside before descending to the small resort of **Brixham** ⓬, where tourism sits alongside a flourishing fishing fleet. The **harbour area** of Brixham has real character, both as a working and leisure port with extensive marina and, in the early morning, a highly active fish market (closed to the public). Moored in the inner harbour is a fine replica of the *Golden Hind* (www.goldenhind.co.uk; mid-Feb–Oct daily 10am–6pm), the ship that took Francis Drake around the world in 1577–80.

The coast road leads up to the last headland in Tor Bay. Grassy **Berry**

Food and Farming

Occombe Farm (Paignton; tel: 01803-520 022; www.countryside-trust.org.uk/occombe; daily 9am–5pm, visitor centre Mon–Fri 9.30am–3.30pm; free) is a working farm aimed at getting adults and kids involved in food and farming, as well as a great place to buy local food. There are nature trails and animals to visit, while year-round events include cookery courses and a special cookery club for children.

A grunt of farmyard piglets.

Berry Head.

Head ⓭, now a nature reserve, boasts the ruins of two forts built in 1803 during the Napoleonic Wars. It's a breezy place where locals walk their dogs, its limestone cliffs home to guillemots – known here as Brixham penguins.

A short drive back and over the headland from here (the steam railway takes the most scenic route) is the town of **Kingswear**, and the more appealing town of **Dartmouth** opposite, a brief ferry ride away (see page 33).

Eating Out

Torquay
The Elephant Restaurant
3–4 Beacon Terrace; tel: 01803-200 044; www.elephantrestaurant.co.uk; Tue–Sat noon–2pm, 6.30–9pm.
With a Michelin star and overlooking Torquay bay, this is fine dining at the highest level. The frequently changing menu champions the best local ingredients. £££
Green Leaf Café
22 Lower Union Lane; tel: 01803-293 207; www.greenleafcafe.co.uk; Mon–Fri 10.30am–2.30pm.
Popular, friendly café serving breakfast, coffee and lunch, including vegan and gluten-free options. £

Babbacombe
The Cary Arms
Babbacombe Beach; tel: 01803-327 110; www.caryarms.co.uk; daily lunch and dinner.

This gastropub is all about a crackling log fire, slow-cooked specials and the lure of a proper pint. Great views. ££

Teignmouth
Jolly Good Fish Café
6 Teign Street; tel: 01626-870 490; Tue–Sat 11.30–9pm, Sun 11.30–6pm
As good as it gets, fish and chips cooked to order and served with a smile. Eat in the cosy café or take it away. £

Brixham
Breakwater Bistro
Berry Head Road; tel: 01803-856 738; www.brixham-restaurant.co.uk; daily breakfast, lunch and dinner, closed dinner Sun–Thu in winter .
Divers, ramblers and beachgoers come for the local mussels and warm crusty bread, paella and crab thermidor. ££

Totnes Castle.

Tour 4

The South Hams

Down the winding lanes on this 71-mile (115km) drive lie nuggets of interest and beauty including one of Devon's finest old towns, Totnes, and the historic port of Dartmouth.

The South Hams is a large, rural area between the Dart and the Tamar rivers, a flowing and verdant beard under the stony face of Dartmoor. The name derives from the old English 'hamme', meaning an enclosed and sheltered place. It has beaches and cliffs, forests and vineyards, deep river valleys and smugglers' coves.

This tour starts just beyond Newton Abbot, at imposing **Ashburton ❶**, north of the A38. Ashburton is a Dartmoor gateway, the largest in the National Park, and one of four strategically placed former stannary towns (with Plympton, Tavistock and Chagford) where tin from mines was weighed and appropriate duty paid. Its tall, wellpreserved 17th- and 18th-century houses reflect the ensuing prosperity.

BUCKFASTLEIGH

Heading south, the Dart broadens considerably, brushing past hidden **Buckfastleigh ❷**. The town had a woollen industry (five mills still operating in 1890) but missed out on the tin wealth of Ashburton, and as a result is on a smaller scale, with small courtyards leading off its narrow main street. The Buckfast Spinning Company at Lower Mills, which used to spin yarn for

Norman tracery on Buckfast Abbey's west entrance.

Axminster carpets a mile (1.5km) upstream from the town, finally closed in 2013. The mill buildings were bought by the Buckfast Abbey Trust and their destiny remains undecided. The mill merges almost seamlessly into the complex of buildings that surround the magnificent **Buckfast Abbey** ❸ (tel: 01364-645 500; www.buckfast.org.uk; Mon–Sat 9am–6pm, Sun noon–6pm; free). The amazing story of Buckfast is well told in an audio-visual exhibition in a converted barn next to the gift shop. The Abbey church itself, Norman in style, has a certain freshness inside and nowhere more so than behind the choir in the Chapel of the Blessed Sacrament (added in 1966), with its glass Christ, arms outstretched.

There is still a small community of industrious monks at Buckfast. When they're not praying they're serving in the shops, bee-keeping or making tonic. Their produce shop uphill from the car park carries a revealing cross section of products from other self-supporting abbeys of Europe.

Between the town and abbey is the **South Devon Railway** ❹ (tel: 01364-644 370; www.southdevonrailway.co.uk; Apr–Oct, see website for winter times), a steam-hauled service that follows the River Dart to Totnes. There's a butterfly farm and otter sanctuary (www.ottersandbutterflies.co.uk) adjacent to Buckfastleigh station.

Dartington Hall, which has the air of a university campus.

DARTINGTON

Travel on the train, however, and you miss the widely scattered **Dartington estate**, 2 miles (3km) north of Totnes. Most visited is the enterprise called **Shops at Dartington**, a group of 14 shops housed in and around a former cider-making building. Much of the high-quality merchandise reflects the Dartington emphasis on arts and crafts, with a particularly good selection of local foods.

This is the commercial side of the Dartington Hall Trust, the creation of philanthropists Leonard and Dorothy Elmhirst, he English and she American, who had in mind a regeneration of rural life when they bought the Hall in 1925. His interest was in agriculture and hers in arts and crafts, and the trust has and continues to be influential county-wide in many guises – the Plough Arts Centre, Dartington Crystal, Morwellham Quay and with its LandWorks programme, providing prisoners support in returning to the community.

For the nerve centre, turn off the A384 by Dartington church and follow it up a slow hill to the arts encampment over the brow, including the Barn Cinema and research centres. Here is **Dartington Hall ❺** (tel: 01803-847 070; www.dartington.org; daily dawn–dusk, visitor centre 9am–5pm free). Built in the 14th century, it has the atmosphere of an Oxbridge college, gathered around a cobbled quad and with a magnificent hammer-beamed Great Hall. Visitors can walk through to view the hall and the gardens beyond, where a variety of sculptures and a grassy-banked amphitheatre are set in mature woodland.

TOTNES

The Dart becomes navigable at **Totnes ❻**, a refined town, frequently described as 'Elizabethan'. In fact its

Retro details at South Devon Railway, Buckfastleigh.

The Guildhall's sturdy pillars, once part of a Benedictine priory.

The face of Totnes has not changed for centuries, stretching up its one main street towards the castle, concealed from view by a tumble of crowding houses. At the river end of this street stands the memorial to William John Wills, a Totnesian who became the first man to cross Australia on foot (1861) and then foolishly tried to retrace his steps. Thereafter a variety of passages and frontages (Totnes Elizabethan House and Museum is at No. 70; mid-Mar–Oct Mon–Fri 10.30am–4pm) is interrupted by the arch of the East Gate across the road, marking the town wall.

known history dates back to AD959, when 'Totta's Ness' (fort on a 'ness', or ridge of ground) was established as a walled town by the kingdom of Wessex. It became a centre for the cloth trade, and in Henry VIII's time was the second-richest town in Devon after Exeter. The port has only recently stopped receiving cargo. As well as history, it has a strong arts culture and is fashionably alternative in an upmarket way, with its own eco project – a move towards a smaller, greener local economy; see www.transitiontowntotnes. org for more information.

A steep right directly under the arch leads up onto the ramparts and round to the **Guildhall** (Apr–Oct Mon–Fri 11am–3pm; donation), a lovely building behind a pillared portico that has its origins in a Benedictine priory of 1088, although the current structure is largely 16th century. The monthly council meeting still gathers around the table where Oliver Cromwell sat in 1646 after taking the town for the Parliamentarians, and the list of mayors dates back to 1359. The main street opens out into the Market Place,

Small streets, small shops, but lots of interesting things to buy.

Shopping in Totnes

Quirky Totnes offers some unusual shops but be warned – some are not cheap. For an ethical pair of handmade leather shoes, which are sustainable and made to fit your feet in the style and colour of your choice, head to Conker Shoe Company, 28 High Street (www.conkershoes.com). Still on the High Street, at No. 1, you'll find Steve Robinson Glass (www.steverobinsonglass.com), which showcases a collection inspired by seascapes and coastal colours.

Haunted Berry Pomeroy Castle.

with the 17th-century granite-pillared **Butterwalk** on one side and rather unfortunate 1960s civic architecture opposite. This is the venue on summer Tuesdays (9am–3pm) for the small Elizabethan market, with traders in period dress.

Turn right at the end of the Butterwalk and within a hundred yards **Totnes Castle** ❼ (tel; 01803-864 406; www.english-heritage.org.uk; Apr–Oct daily 10am–5pm, with exceptions, Nov–Mar Sat–Sun 10am–4pm) looms overhead. This is a plain but perfectly preserved Norman motte and bailey structure, whose simplicity adds to its power. One way the eye travels over

The old Butterwalk has an original interior and a few ghosts.

crowded rooftops, and the other it climbs up onto Dartmoor.

A diversion out of Totnes just off the Paignton road (A385) is **Berry Pomeroy Castle**, a romantic ruin with pleasant woodland walks, but with a reputation as Devon's most haunted castle. The A381 from Totnes to Dartmouth is slow and winding, and there are plenty of potential diversions en route such as the Sharpham vineyard at **Ashprington**, with walks and tastings. From Ashpring-

Dartmouth's Historic Centre

The granite-pillared 17th-century **Butterwalk** in Duke Street is well preserved and forms part of the Dartmouth Museum (6a The Butterwalk; tel: 01803-832 923; www.dartmouthmuseum.org; Easter–Oct Sun–Mon 1–4pm, Tue–Sat 10am–4pm, Nov–Easter 1–4pm). Supposedly haunted, it showcases marine artefacts, shipping, shipbuilding and the Henley study, a child-friendly Victorian experience. Just up here, past the crossroads with pedestrianised Foss Street, is the solid old market, built around a cobbled square in 1828.

ton a road heads southeast through Tuckenhay, down to the shore-side village of **Dittisham** (home to a few retired millionaires), with great views and a passenger ferry across the Dart. Known by the locals as "Ditsum", there are a couple of pubs, the Red Lion and the Ferry Boat Inn, in which to stop for refreshment.

DARTMOUTH

Nicely sheltered on the west bank at the end of the Dart estuary, the town of **Dartmouth** ❽ is truly delightful. It faces the small town of **Kingswear** (vehicle and passenger ferries run year round, see box opposite). The waters are thick with boats in one of Britain's best anchorages. Dartmouth has a long maritime history and a strong Navy presence on its shores and back up the hill above the town, where the **Britannia Royal Naval College** puts would-be officers, including many in the Royal Family, through their paces.

Dartmouth is focused on the **Boat Float** – an inner harbour full of dinghies – and the streets that run off it, crowded with historic buildings whose fine frontages are decorated with painted heads, coats of arms, and stained and leaded glass.

Outer Froward Point

If you take one boat trip, be sure it's the one over to Kingswear, home to the Royal Dart Yacht Club – whose main attraction is its view, especially in the late afternoon. It is a 3-mile (5km) walk to Outer Froward Point from where there is a magical view of Dartmouth and the Dart estuary with its castles and cliffs. From Kingswear railway station walk downhill then turn left up the Alma Steps. At the top turn right and follow the coastal path signs. More details at www.southwestcoastpath.org.uk.

A pleasant bandstand and garden where palm trees testify to the gentle climate occupy one side of the Float. The **Tourist Information Office** is in the same building as a small exhibition housing a working steam engine to commemorate Thomas Newcomen, inventor, who was born in Dartmouth in 1663.

On the promenade between the Float and the estuary stands the restaurant and champagne bar, Platform 1 The Station, on the site of what was Britain's only station

The Boat Float is at the heart of the town of Dartmouth.

The South West Coast Path is 630 miles (1,013km) long.

without tracks: passengers would buy their train tickets here then hop on the ferry across to Kingswear, where the steam train from Paignton runs right down to the quay. The passenger ferry still runs.

Returning to quay level and heading away from the Float, it's a short walk to **Bayards Cove**, by the ferry landing. Bayards is less of a cove and more a well-preserved shore front, and has appeared as the backdrop to many films. At the end of the short prom is a walk-in artillery fort built by Dartmouth Corporation in 1510, where high tide laps right up to the gunholes.

Bigger fortifications are a mile or so further south. **Dartmouth Castle** ❾ (tel: 01803-833 588; www.

Dinghies moored in picturesque Salcombe harbour.

english-heritage.org.uk; Apr–Oct daily 10am–5pm, with exceptions, Nov–Mar Sat–Sun 10am–4pm), clamped to a shoulder of rock where the Dart meets the sea, is three elements: the original castle (1481), St Petrock's church (1642, although a church has been here since the 12th century) and a Victorian artillery fort.

The best way to see these castles and the Dart estuary is on a **boat trip**. Hidden creeks, imposing private houses, birdlife and sloping vineyards line its navigable 12 miles (19km) to Totnes. Boat is also the best way of reaching **Greenway** (NT; tel: 01803-842 382; Mar–Oct daily 10.30am–5pm, Nov–Dec Sat–Sun 11am–4pm). This lovely waterside property was the holiday home of Agatha Christie and her husband Max, from 1938 to 1959.

Heading south from Dartmouth on the A379, the cliffs drop away first to **Blackpool Sands**, a delightful golden curve of a beach, fairly undeveloped despite its name, before running along the broad shingle at **Slapton Ley**, where an inland freshwater lake is thick with birds. US forces trained here for the Normandy landings of 1944, and locals had to leave their houses. The road dives inland here, but there is a fine cliff walk to **Start Point** via the remains of a village that has crumbled into the sea at Hallsands. From Torcross, continue on the A379 and head west.

Kingsbridge and Salcombe, respectively at the head and mouth of a 5-mile (8km) sea inlet, mirror Totnes and Dartmouth, although on a smaller scale. The steep main street at **Kingsbridge** ❿ is reminiscent of Totnes, as are its passages – find the aptly named Squeezebelly Lane just to the left of the Hermitage Inn. Its former town hall, incorporating the Kings Cinema, has a clock with three

The curvy shingle beach at Blackpool Sands.

faces: the fourth side is blank, because it once faced the workhouse. At the top of the hill is the Shambles, an old market hall raised on 16th-century granite pillars.

A leisurely drive south on the A381 will take you through lovely countryside. The sailing clippers at **Salcombe** ⓫ used to bring back the first fruit harvest from the Caribbean. Now this attractive fishing village, snug with lovely pubs, is a yachting centre, its narrow streets bursting at weekends. Sandy bays on the other side of the inlet are a short ferry ride from the town quay.

North from Salcombe, rejoin the A379. The coastline westwards from here is one of shipwrecks and secret smugglers' coves. Inland is a hidden rural landscape that repays exploration.

After the handsome 18th-century town of **Modbury**, it is a short drive to Plymouth (see page 38).

Eating Out

Dartington
The White Hart
Dartington Hall; tel: 01803-847 111; www.dartington.org; daily lunch and dinner.
Set in a medieval hall with Gothic chandeliers and ancient tapestries, this is an elegant place to enjoy local venison and freshwater trout. Fifty percent of produce used is sourced within 20 miles (32 km). ££

Totnes
The Wild Fig
53 Fore Street; tel: 01803-864 829; www.thewildfig.co.uk; Mon–Sat 8.30am–5pm.
This welcoming and intimate café serves ethical and locally sourced food. Everything is homemade – choose from salads, baguettes, wraps and seasonal specials, plus superb coffee. £

Dartmouth
Anzac Street Bistro
Anzac Street; tel: 01803-835 515; www.anzacbistro.co.uk; Tue–Sat 6–10pm.
You'll find an interesting mix of flavours here, where Mediterranean dishes are produced with a Polish twist. Vegetarian options such as goat cheese and beetroot risotto feature on the menu. ££

The Seahorse
5 South Embankment; tel: 01803-835 147; www.seahorserestaurant.co.uk; Tue–Sat lunch, dinner, Sun lunch only.
Fabulous local fish and seafood cooked fresh off the boats over an open charcoal fire. Expensive, but the setting on the banks of the River Dart justifies the cost. £££

Salcombe
The Sun Bay Restaurant
Inner Hope Cove; tel: 01548-561 371; www.sunbayhotel-hopecove.co.uk; daily lunch and dinner.
Overlooking the rugged coastline and sandy beaches of Hope Cove, this place offers line-caught fish and crab from local fishermen, plus delicious traditional and savoury cream teas. Children are welcome. ££

Literary Devon

Devon has inspired a host of literary greats and some classic tales. Some authors were born here, others settled here, finding inspiration in the county's landscape.

Soft light and outstanding landscapes have long provided fuel for the creative mind. They have also given Devon a literary heritage that's fun to follow as you tour the county.

HOMEGROWN TALENT

One of the most enduring classics of the county is RD Blackmore's highly romantic *Lorna Doone*, published in 1869, much filmed and never out of print. This 17th-century epic has given a new label to the upper East Lyn – the Doone Valley. Blackmore had the valley of Lank Combe in mind as the home of his outlaw family, the Doones (based on real Exmoor outlaws, the Gubbins), although the Malmsmead valley has since taken over the title.

Also a strong crowd-puller – even bringing the Japanese to Torquay – is Britain's most prolific author, Agatha Christie. Born in Torquay in 1890, Christie spent much of her lifetime in the area. She wrote two of her books while staying in the Art Deco hotel on Burgh Island. Her house, Greenway (see page 34), on the banks of the Dart, is pointed out by pleasure-boat captains and there are exhibitions devoted to the writer in Torre Abbey and Torquay Museum.

Charles Kingsley, author of *The Water Babies*, was born in the Dartmoor

Fear stalks the Moors as Christopher Lee confronts the Hound of the Baskervilles

John Gay, poet and author of the *Beggar's Opera*, was born in Barnstaple in 1685, and went to school in the charismatic St Anne's Chapel, where a small exhibition preserves some of the atmosphere of the time.

INSPIRING DEVON

Many more giants of literature came here seeking inspiration. Arthur Conan Doyle visited Dartmoor, and used the name of his coachman-guide – Baskerville – in *The Hound of the Baskervilles*. Rudyard Kipling based *Stalky and Co.* on his college life in Bideford.

Other writers and poets simply used Devon as a peaceful place for the creative process. Evelyn Waugh wrote *Brideshead Revisited* while staying in a hotel near Chagford, and John Galsworthy wrote *The Forsyte Saga* while living on a farm at Manaton, on the eastern side of Dartmoor.

In tourism terms, the biggest impact has been made by Henry Williamson, who came to settle in Georgeham, near Croyde. His are the most telling footprints on the landscape, thanks to the book and film of *Tarka the Otter*. Much of Mid Devon has been dubbed 'Tarka Country', with key points from the book along the Tarka Trail.

The poet laureate, Ted Hughes, who moved to North Tawton in 1961 and lived there until his death in 1998, loved and wrote about Devon's countryside. At his request, his ashes were scattered on Dartmoor. Hilary Mantel, two-time winner of the Man Booker Prize for her Tudor novels *Wolf Hall* and *Bring up the Bodies*, was first drawn to Devon as a child. She finally moved to Budleigh Salterton in 2011 where she is Honorary President of the town's prestigious annual literary festival.

village of Holne in 1819, although he is more closely associated with the North Devon coast, particularly Clovelly, where his father was vicar, and Bideford, where the name Westward Ho! is named after one of his books.

Samuel Taylor Coleridge was born in 1772 in Ottery St Mary, where his father was rector, and although he spent most of his life elsewhere, he never lost his Devon accent. In later years the poet Robert Southey and Coleridge would carouse in the Ship Inn at Porlock Weir; and it was an unknown person from Porlock who so rudely interrupted the narrator in *Kubla Khan*.

Tour 5

Plymouth and the Tamar Valley

Explore the naval city of Plymouth, then head north to the edge of wild Dartmoor. At Tavistock, cross the river Tamar to Cornwall on this full-day, 70-mile (112km) drive.

The largest city in Devon, and a major naval base, **Plymouth ❶** (pop. approximately 262,000) was so damaged in the last war it is mostly a new town. It was once three townships: Dock (now Devonport), Sutton and Stonehouse. The natural harbour, formed where the Tamar and Plym rivers debouch into the Sound, was already a significant port in the 14th century, controlling the English Channel. Numerous discoverers and pioneers set off on their epic voyages from here: Drake, Hawkins, Raleigh, Cook, the Pilgrim Fathers and half a million emigrants.

One night in 1941, 1,000 people were killed and 20,000 homes destroyed by German bombs. After the war, town planners scrapped what remained and started again. The result is a pedestrian shopping centre surrounded by traffic.

Although it is only a few miles from the downtown stores to the bleak uplands of Dartmoor, the contrast couldn't be greater.

Highlights

- Plymouth Hoe
- Buckland Abbey
- Launceston
- Morwellham Quay
- Antony House
- Mount Edgcumbe House

Smeaton's Tower, now high and dry on the Hoe, once stood on a rock far out to sea.

THE HOE

The setting for many of Plymouth's best dramas is **The Hoe** Ⓐ (old English for 'high place'), a broad, breezy, grassy shoulder between town and sea. It commands an extraordinary view of the Sound, laid out below like an amphitheatre. This is where Sir Francis Drake was alleged to have been playing bowls when the Spanish Armada arrived in 1588.

In the far distance (14 miles/23km), the Eddystone lighthouse can be seen on a clear day. The current lighthouse is the fourth; the third, **Smeaton's Tower**, now stands on the Hoe, and is open to the public daily 10am–5pm.

Several memorials line the Hoe leading to the formidable walls of the **Royal Citadel** Ⓑ. The fort was completed in 1671 by Charles II, shortly after Plymouth had taken the anti-royalist side in the Civil War, and its guns face both ways – over the city and the sea – although they have never been fired in anger. The Citadel is garrisoned by the Royal Artillery.

Well landscaped into the front brow of the Hoe is the **Dome**, a former innovative multi-media presentation of Plymouth's past and present, which is now an Italian restaurant, Villa Amaranta.

Plymouth's old Aquarium used to be here, but has since been reborn as the grand **National Marine Aquarium** Ⓒ (tel: 0844-893 7938; www.national-aquarium.co.uk; daily, daily 10am–5pm) on the east side of Sutton Harbour. It's the largest aquarium in the UK.

Sutton Harbour is the watery part of the **Barbican** Ⓓ, a preserved corner of Plymouth as it used to be, from where many of Plymouth's historic voyages started out. The tourist information office here houses the Mayflower Museum, which showcases the story of the Pilgrim Fathers' voyage across the Atlantic. The Barbican's shops, restaurants and galleries are attractively located in converted warehouses and merchants' houses, particularly along Southside Street. Towards the end of the street you'll find the **Plymouth Gin Distillery** (www.plymouthdistillery.com), which welcomes visitors for tours.

Plymouth is a city without a cathedral. **St Andrew's** Ⓔ, its principal church, was largely rebuilt following the war, and is notable for striking glass windows by artist John Piper, as well as graffiti scratched into the masonry which is thought to celebrate Drake's voyage round the world.

The **Plymouth City Museum and Art Gallery** ⓕ, behind the main shopping area on Drake Circus, is currently closed for redevelopment but is set to re-open in spring 2020 as part of **The Box**, a major cultural and heritage attraction where the museum and five other collections will come together under one roof.

DEVON WONDERS

Just off the A38 3 miles (5km) east of Plymouth stands the grand **Saltram House** ❷ (NT; tel: 01752-333 500; house: Mar–Oct daily noon–4.30pm, 21 Nov–23 Dec noon–8pm, mid-Jan– end Feb 11am–3.30pm; park all year dawn–dusk), Devon's largest country house, in 470 acres (190 hectares) of grounds and 13 acres (5.3 hectares) of gardens. It has a fine Robert Adam interior and most of its furnishings are original. The house served as the Dashwood family home in the film of *Sense and Sensibility*.

The River Tamar

Nothing has done more to keep Cornwall Cornish than the River Tamar. From its springs at Woolley Barrows, just a few miles from the north Cornish coast, down to Plymouth Sound, it proved an effective barrier against the Romans and the Anglo Saxons, and provided broad waters and landing places for the ships that took away the produce of Cornish mines (copper and tin) and its quarries (granite and slate).

Some 8 miles (13km) north of Plymouth, just off the A386 en route to Tavistock, are two West Devon highlights. **Buckland Abbey** ❸ (NT; tel: 01822-853 607; mid-Feb– Oct daily 11am–5pm, Nov–Dec until 4pm) belonged to the Cistercian order and dates from 1278. Dissolved under Henry VIII, it became a wonderful Elizabethan mansion, and home of Drake, who was born in nearby Tavistock. He bought the house in 1580 from his rival Sir Richard Grenville for £3,400.

Saltram House has year-round events, exhibitions and activities.

Beautifully-preserved Morwellham Quay shows how copper was transported on the Tamar.

Four miles (6km) north is **Morwellham Quay** ❹ (tel: 01822-832 766; www.morwellham-quay.co.uk; daily 10am–5pm, closes 4pm Nov–Feb), the highest navigable point on the Tamar. Morwellham is a superbly preserved and presented snapshot of how industry and thus transport ebbed and flowed in the region in Victorian times. It is set in a lovely valley, and animated by staff in period costume.

Morwellham existed as a port for a thousand years before the discovery of huge copper deposits in the region demanded the provision of heavy transport – so much so that a canal was cut from Tavistock to the hills above Morwellham, from where an inclined railway ran down to the quay. Eventually the mines were exhausted and the railway arrived, killing off water transport. Morwellham disappeared under weeds until 1970, when it became a project of the Dartington Trust, which lovingly restored and created its museums and trails.

TAVISTOCK

The pleasant old market town of **Tavistock** ❺ benefited enormously from the prosperity of local copper and tin mining. The landowning Russell family (dukes of Bedford) created the town as it looks today, particularly the main Bedford Square. Plunge through the arch near the tourist office and you will reach the town's active and characterful pannier market. Tavistock is only 10

Launceston Castle

Launceston Castle (Apr–Oct daily 10am–5pm) sits in grounds immaculately maintained by English Heritage. The steep ascent to the keep is worthwhile for the astounding views from the top – not only of the town but also over Bodmin Moor and Dartmoor. William the Conqueror gave his half-brother, the Earl of Mortain, the land surrounding a hill site already fortified by Edward the Confessor and commanding the approaches to the west. Within a year the hill was crowned with the castle of Dunheved, a keep on an artificial motte, with bailey, walls and gates enclosing the settlement. Launceston was born, secure from English resistance. A small display traces the castle's 1,000 years of history.

A lofty castle keep.

North of the centre is the **Launceston Steam Railway** (tel: 01566-775 665; www.launcestonsr. co.uk for hours and timetable; not Sat or winter). There is a museum, workshops and buffet and the old locomotives run 2.5 miles (4km) to Newmills.

THE TAMAR VALLEY

From Launceston, the A388, the major road south, deserts the Tamar, but our tour turns left at St Mellion and winds its way through pretty lanes to **Cotehele Quay** ❼. Evidence of a once-busy trading place is captured in a museum, wharf buildings and the *Shamrock*, the last Tamar sailing barge. There's a National Trust tearoom, a watermill and recreated workshops just a short walk through the woods.

The complex relates to **Cotehele House** (NT; tel: 01579-351 346; daily mid-Mar–Oct 11am–4pm, Nov & Dec parts of the house are open; garden all year dawn–dusk), a strong contender for the title of most beautiful stately home in the county. Built between 1485 and 1627, this great medieval building, hung with Flemish and English tapestries, is remarkably unchanged. In the chapel, a 15th-century clock, the earliest in

miles (16km) from Plymouth, but with its weathered stone buildings it belongs to another world.

LAUNCESTON

Take the B3362 about 12 miles (19km) northwest to **Launceston** ❻. Just 1 mile (1.6km) before the walled city you will cross the River Tamar into the county of Cornwall.

Launceston was Cornwall's principal town until civic power was transferred to Bodmin in 1835. A Victorian revival gave it a town hall and a guildhall, but its most interesting building is **St Mary Magdalene**, once the castle chapel and now the parish church. Go out via the North Gate into elegant 18th-century Castle Street. **Lawrence House Museum** (www.law rencehousemuseum.org.uk; Apr–Oct Mon–Fri 10.30am–4pm; free) was originally built in 1753 for a lawyer.

Set in vast grounds, Cotehele House has a wonderful textile collection.

England, still ticks, though it has no hands or pendulum.

A short riverside walk brings you to **Calstock ⑧**. River trade was ruined when the Tamar Valley railway line between Plymouth and Gunnislake was laid, but it gave the town one of the county's most attractive branch lines. The views of the river from the viaduct are breathtaking.

Until Victorian times **Gunnislake**, several miles upriver from Calstock, was the lowest bridging point on the Tamar. New Bridge, dating from 1520, was the scene of bitter fighting during the Civil War (1642–6).

SALTASH

Return to the A388 and drive south to **Saltash ⑨**. Isambard Kingdom Brunel's magnificent Royal Albert Bridge straddled the Tamar in 1859 here, to bring broad-gauge railways into Cornwall, 9 miles (15km) south of Gunnislake. Not until 1961 did a new road bridge join Brunel's, forcing the closure of a ferry that had operated for 700 years. The new A38 took traffic around Saltash, leaving it to rest on its memories, the oldest ones embedded in the tiny Tudor cottage in Culver Road, where Sir Francis Drake's wife

Mary was born, **Mary Newman's Cottage** (Easter–Oct Wed–Thu, Sat–Sun, noon–4pm; free), and Elliott's Grocery Store, a classic Saltash shop.

Stunning views can be had from below the bridge, where 18th-century houses cluster side by side with modern housing in the steep streets and on the quayside.

ST GERMANS

From Saltash, take the A38 westwards. High above a tidal creek of the Lynher River is **Trematon Castle**, an important Norman stronghold overlooking Plymouth Sound.

Launceston Steam Railway runs along the lovely Kensey Valley.

In Saxon times, the church at **St Germans** ⑩, reached via a narrow left turn off the A38, was Cornwall's cathedral. After the bishops moved to Crediton, and later Exeter, it became an Augustinian priory, and the substantial remains of the Norman building are now the parish church.

TWO GREAT HOUSES

The A38 joins the A374 to Torpoint and the Devonport ferry, passing **Antony House** ⑪ (NT; tel: 01752-812 191; Apr–Oct Tue–Thu 12.30–4.30pm, also Sun June–Aug), by the River Lynher. Wings of red brick contrast with Pentewan stone and, although a little austere, it is one of the finest early 18th-century houses in Cornwall. Views of the river have been opened up in the 100-acre (40-hectare) park and woodland garden, landscaped by Humphry Repton.

From Antony House, head back to the main road junction and follow signs south for **Millbrook**. From the village, at the head of a tidal creek, a delightful lane follows the waterside to **Mount Edgcumbe House** ⑫ (tel: 01752-822 236; www.mountedgcumbe.gov.

Brunel bridged the Tamar for the railways; the road bridge came later.

uk; Apr–Sept Sun–Thu 11am–4.30pm) and the entrance to the Country Park at Cremyll Ferry. The Edgcumbe family virtually abandoned their original home at Cotehele in favour of this new site overlooking Plymouth Sound.

Entrance to the 800-acre (320-hectare) park (all year daily) is free; it includes Cornwall's only Grade I listed historic garden, the National Camellia Collection, follies, grottoes, an orangery, a conservatory and a holy well.

There are dramatic coastal views from walks that lead to **Maker**

Animal Rescue

Two children's animal favourites are accessible from Launceston. About 14 miles (22km) southeast is **Tamar Valley Donkey Park and Sanctuary** (tel: 01822-834 072; www.donkeypark.com; Apr–Sept daily 10.30am–5pm, Oct Thu–Sun 10.30am–4.30pm, Nov–Mar Sat–Sun and school holidays). While north, off the A390 near Callington, you'll find the **Tamar Otter Sanctuary** (tel: 01566-785 646; www.tamarotters.co.uk; Apr–Oct daily 10.30am–6pm), plus meerkats, wallabies, wildcats and birds of prey.

Otters awaiting rehabilitation.

The church of St Germans, a former priory and once Cornwall's cathedral.

Church, the tower of which served as a semaphore station in the 18th century. The coastal path soon descends to **Kingsand** and **Cawsand**, separated by a stream. In the early 19th century both subsisted on smuggling, for which their twisting, turning lanes seem to have been specially designed. From here it is just a short hop over the Tamar Bridge to Plymouth.

Eating Out

Plymouth
Quay 33
33 Southside Street; tel: 01752-229 345; www.quay33.co.uk; Mon–Sat lunch and dinner.
Kick back and relax while enjoying well-crafted British and Mediterranean cuisine cooked by Chef Dave Morgan at his popular restaurant with views over Sutton Harbour. ££

The Waterfront
9 Grand Parade; tel: 01752-226 961; www.waterfront-plymouth.co.uk; daily 9am–11pm, closes 10.30pm Sun.
Sit on the nautical deck on the Hoe and start with moules marinere cooked in garlic followed by local pork and leek sausages. ££

Tavistock
The Cornish Arms
15 West Street; tel: 01822-612 145; www.thecornisharmstavistock.co.uk; daily lunch, dinner.
Exceptional food and beer can be found in this stylish, yet traditional pub. Chef John Hooker produces top-notch dishes using great local produce, such as Sladesdown duck from Ashburton. ££

Launceston
No. 8 Café & Deli
8 Westgate Street; tel: 01566-777 369; www.no8launceston.co.uk; Mon–Sat 8.30am–5pm.
Come here for a taste of Cornwall, in particular the great cream teas and the very popular breakfasts. Good coffee, sandwiches and salads, too. £

Saltash
Heskyn Mill
Tideford (just off A38 west of Saltash); tel: 01752-852 127; www.heskyn-mill.co.uk; Tue–Sat lunch and dinner, Sun lunch.
In a delightful setting within an 18th-century corn mill, the food here is lovingly prepared and the service is attentive. Leave room for the luscious desserts. ££

Sunset over Staple Tor.

Tour 6

Dartmoor

One of Britain's great wilderness areas, Dartmoor is a high and haunting place. This 69-mile (111km) full-day drive reveals its mysteries and rugged grandeur.

Dartmoor National Park covers some 365 sq miles (945 sq km) of south-central Devon. Although the moor is governed by the park authority, the land is still largely in private hands. Prince Charles, title holder of the Duchy of Cornwall, is the largest single landowner. Look out for the Dartmoor ponies who have roamed here freely since the 10th century.

Reaching 2,037ft (621m), the moor is the highest land in southern England. Around half of it is open moorland, and the rest (particularly on the eastern side) is steep wooded valleys with secluded villages.

Dartmoor generates a climate of its own. In the distant past this climate was kinder, and the high moor was more heavily cultivated and populated than

Highlights

- Hay Tor
- Princetown
- Okehampton Castle views
- Museum of Dartmoor Life, Okehampton
- Lydford Gorge

it is today. The first people worked the moor 10,000 years ago, and until 7,000 years ago it was mostly wooded. But as the climate worsened, so the population left their settlements in search of easier ground lower down. As a result, Dartmoor has a wealth of around 2,000 Bronze Age sites – hut circles, tombs and ceremonial stones – dating from around 4,000BC. Mixed in with Bronze

National Trust

If you are keen on visiting stately homes and, especially, gardens, it is worth considering becoming a National Trust member. Many of the houses and gardens described en route (those marked NT), and more besides, are in the care of the Trust. You could soon recoup your membership fee as well as contributing to the upkeep not only of the properties, but of much of the coast that is also under the Trust's protection.

Contact them at tel: 0344-800 1895, or www.nationaltrust.org.uk, or fill in a form and join on the spot when visiting any of their properties.

Age remnants are signs of more recent industry, in particular the mining of tin, granite and copper from the 12th to 19th centuries.

Tin mining – largely tin streaming in the open river beds – was a boom industry, and the Dartmoor miners were granted special exemption from the nation's taxes. Although they never numbered more than a few hundred, they made a powerful group with their own laws, their own parliament (which met at Crockern Tor) and their own judiciary and prison at Lydford. Their contribution to the nation's coffers was made at the strategically placed stannary towns of Ashburton, Chagford, Plympton and Tavistock; here the tin was weighed and duty paid.

Strange legends and traditions persist, including the pastime of letterboxing, a sort of moorland treasure hunt (see page 50); and as recently as the mid-19th century, if you could build a house on Dartmoor between sunrise and sunset, it and the land were yours.

Since Napoleonic times, areas have been assigned for military use. On firing days, warning flags fly around restricted areas (a PDF of the firing schedules can be downloaded at www.gov.uk/government/publications/dartmoor-firing-programme).

BOVEY TRACEY

The eastern gateway to the moor is **Bovey Tracey ❶**, a pleasant, small town with a long main street heading up the hillside. It was the scene of an undignified fracas during the Civil War when Royalists were surprised at cards, but managed to escape by scattering their stake money, which proved too much

Bovey Crafts

Bovey's solid granite architecture is unremarkable, but it does have two shopping highlights. In a small industrial estate on the Exeter side of town **The House of Marbles and Teign Valley Glassworks** (www. houseofmarbles.com) has glass and pottery in a synthesis of museum and retailing, with some glass-blowing on site. Further towards the centre of town is the **Devon Guild of Craftsmen**, located in an appealing old riverside 'mill' (actually a stable block with a waterwheel to pump water for the horses), with exhibition space on the first floor. The range and quality of the Devon Guild's members is extremely high, but prices can be steep; www.crafts.org.uk.

Pottery and glass items for sale.

of a temptation for Cromwell's impoverished troops.

From Bovey, head west towards Widecombe. Just outside town is **Parke House**, headquarters of the Dartmoor National Park Authority. At this point a short diversion northwest

St Pancras in Widecombe, the Cathedral of the Moor.

towards Manaton brings you to **Becky Falls ❷** (www.beckyfalls.com), more a dramatic series of tumbles than a waterfall, with tearoom and nature trails in very pleasant woodland.

TO WIDECOMBE

Back on the Widecombe road, the climb is steep, and the moor opens out at the popular **Hay Tor ❸** (1,491ft/450m), with far-reaching views. It is a short and relatively easy walk from the road to the great granite tor (rock). Running along the back shoulder of the hill is the **Granite Tramway**, a track made from granite, with points, that was used to transport granite from the quarry in the hillside 10 miles (16km) down to the Stover canal. To the northwest is **Hound Tor**, and in the valley on the far side are evident remains of a medieval village among the bracken.

Widecombe-in-the-Moor ❹ is a small, captivating place superbly situated in a deep trough but still 800ft (240m) above sea level. Its outsized church of St Pancras is known as the Cathedral of the Moor. The town has become a tourist attraction thanks to the song about its annual fair. It dates from the 1860s, and was intended to attract 'Uncle Tom Cobley and all' away from similar events elsewhere. Such is the power of advertising that the September fair remains

Eerie and impenetrable Dartmoor Prison, whose museum gives a glimpse of life inside.

a major celebration, with country skills and livestock competitions.

Down narrow lanes south of Widecombe are two other pretty Dartmoor villages. **Buckland-in-the-Moor**, although scattered around a wooded hillside, has one of the most photographed groups of thatched cottages in Devon. The small church has an unusual clock face with the 12 letters my dear mother instead of numerals. Further south is **Holne**, birthplace of *The Water Babies* author Charles Kingsley. The 14th-century Church House Inn is one of Dartmoor's most characterful.

From Widecombe the main road heads west through the surprisingly popular spot of Dartmeet and thence up to Two Bridges. Both locations are little more than their names suggest: the former is the meeting place for the East and West Dart rivers, and the latter is a hotel next to old and new river crossings.

PRINCETOWN

Princetown ⑤, the highest and bleakest settlement on Dartmoor, shelters beneath the huge transmitter mast on North Hessary Tor. It has the grim aspect of a frontier town, and in bad weather is regularly cut off. Amazingly, a railway reached here from Plymouth in 1883, but was closed in 1956.

After the mast, the town's landmark is **Dartmoor Prison**, built in 1806 for French prisoners of the Napoleonic Wars. After the introduction of deportation to the colonies it stood empty for many years, but today it functions as one of Britain's maximumsecurity prisons. A small **museum** (tel: 01822-322 130; www.dartmoor-prison.co.uk; open daily 9.30am–4.30pm, Fri & Sat until 4pm, closed Jan) charts its history, and has some items confiscated over the years.

Stories and legends

By Princetown's central crossroads is the **National Park Visitor Centre** (tel: 01822-890 414; www.dartmoor.

Devon thatch at Buckland-in-the-Moor.

The Three Crowns at Chagford is supposedly haunted by a Royalist poet who died in its porch.

gov.uk; Mar–Oct daily 10am–5pm, Nov–Feb Tue–Sun 10.30am–3.30pm, free) with beautiful displays on Dartmoor's history and wildlife and insights into some of its legends. This is also the place to find out about the schedule of guided walks.

Across the road you'll find the ancient pub, **Plume of Feathers**, the oldest building in the area (1795). During a refreshment stop here, you can ponder the story of the fearful winter wayfarer who opened a box seat in his

The old market hall, Chagford.

room to discover the body of a man. Murder was assumed, until the landlord confessed that the body was that of his father, and he was only being stored there while the ground remained too hard to be dug.

From Princetown return northeast to Two Bridges and then north for **Postbridge**. This straight stretch of road has fuelled one of Dartmoor's best-known legends. A pair of hairy hands is reputed to have caused several accidents by appearing from nowhere and wresting control of the steering wheel. The 14th-century bridge at Postbridge, made from vast granite slabs, is the best example of a traditional local 'clapper' bridge. The moor softens as the road continues northeast to **Moretonhampstead**, an attractive small town blighted by the five roads that meet in the town centre. Moreton has become something of an arts and crafts centre, with a number of studios and potteries. On the way out of town are Moreton's

Letterboxers get a stamp to show they passed this way.

almshouses, dating from 1637 and now the property of the National Trust.

CHAGFORD

Chagford ❻ lies a short distance northwest, off the A382 to Okehampton. Its stannary past has left the town looking remarkably elegant, gathered around a small market square at the centre of which is the six-sided and spired Market House (1862), known locally as the Pepperpot. Shopping around the square is a mixture of art galleries and arts and crafts. Off the top left-hand corner of the square is the 16th-century **Three Crowns** inn, which is supposedly haunted by the Cavalier poet,

Sydney Godolphin, who was fatally shot here.

Back on the road to Okehampton, the silhouette of **Castle Drogo** ❼ (NT; tel: 01647-433 306; Mar–Oct 11am–5pm, visitor centre and grounds also open Feb, Nov & Dec) looms ahead up on the hill to the right, although the journey to its door is about 3 miles (4.8km) through narrow lanes. This dramatic situation was chosen by one Julius Drewe while picnicking here with his family. The last castle to be built in England, in 1910, it was designed by Edwin Lutyens and has plenty of features, including tapestries from the 17th century. At pres-

Hilltop Castle Drogo commands impressive views.

Mural in Okehampton depicting a man of the moor.

ent covered in scaffolding, the building is undergoing major refurbishment (due to finish sometime in 2019) and some of the interiors are inaccessible but remains open to the public.

Outside are terraced gardens and woodland walks down into the Teign Gorge. Particularly worthwhile is the walk to **Fingle Bridge**, a 400-year-old footbridge of some charm a couple of miles upstream, which can also be reached by road via the pretty hilltop village of **Drewsteignton**.

Just before Okehampton, in Sticklepath, is the **Finch Foundry ❽** (NT; tel: 01837-840 046; early Mar–Oct daily 11am–5pm, Nov & Dec Sat–Sun until 3pm), remarkable because it was still manufacturing edged tools by hand as recently as 1960, using hammers, shears and grindstones powered by waterwheels – all still in working order. Local farmers swear by their Finch tools.

OKEHAMPTON

The A30 sweeps past the market town of **Okehampton ❾**, cutting it off from the moor to which it spiritually belongs. The town is a matter-of-fact sort of place, and is particularly well served by the **Museum of Dartmoor Life** (tel: 01837-52295; www.dartmoorlife.org.uk; Easter–Oct Mon–Fri 10.15am–4.15pm, Sat 10.15am–1pm, shorter hours in winter), found through an arch off the main street. The museum gives

detailed insights into the archaeology and sociology of the moor, with good use of aerial photography.

Okehampton's **Castle** (Apr–Nov 10am–5pm, Jul–Aug until 6pm) has been a ruin since Henry VIII seized it in 1538, but what it lacks in roof it makes up for in location, on a hilltop in a wooded valley half a mile behind the museum, and with a riverside picnic area below. The castle was built in 1068 by Baldwin de Brionne, the first sheriff of Devon.

GORGE AND WATERFALL

Return to the A30 and then take the moor-skirting A386 south. Half way to Tavistock, off to the right, is the village of **Lydford**, a former administrative centre of the Royal Forest of Dartmoor whose castle is actually just a prison keep. The earth thrown up around it gives it the appearance of a castle.

Gidleigh Park dessert.

The scenic **Lydford Gorge** (NT; tel: 01822-820 320; Mar–Sept daily 10am–5pm, Oct 10am–4pm, Nov–Dec 10am–3.30pm) is just beyond the village. The River Lyd thunders through it, shadowed by an alarming walkway. In more gentle scenery downstream the river is joined by the elegant White Lady Waterfall, which is actually more a slide than a fall.

The last stop on this route, **Brent Tor** , can be reached either via back lanes from Lydford or by returning to the A386. From here it is a short distance to Tavistock (see page 41).

The White Lady Waterfall in scenic Lydford Gorge.

Eating Out

Widecombe-in-the-Moor
Rugglestone Inn
tel: 01364-621 327; www.rugglestoneinn.co.uk; daily lunch and dinner.
Sample good home-cooked fare washed down by a real ale or local farm cider at this pretty stone pub near the centre of Widecombe. It's wise to book in high season. £

Bovey Tracey
The Old Pottery
The House of Marbles; tel: 01626-831 320; www.houseofmarbles.com; Mon–Sat 9am–4.30pm, Sun 10am–4.30pm.
Located in The House of Marbles and Teign Valley Glassworks, this locals' favourite serves excellent breakfast and Devon cream teas. Salads, sandwiches and traditional mains also feature. £

Princetown
The Plume of Feathers Inn
Yelverton; tel: 01822-890 240; www.theplumeoffeathersdartmoor.co.uk; daily lunch and dinner.
This atmospheric inn has a frequently changing menu with local Dartmoor meats from an award-winning butcher, and fresh Devon vegetables. There is also a carvery on Sundays, as well as a beer garden and a large, safe, fenced-in adventure play area. £

Chagford
Gidleigh Park
tel: 01647-432 367; www.gidleigh.co.uk/restaurant; daily lunch, afternoon tea and dinner.
This property, a favourite with foodies, enjoys an idyllic setting on the banks of the North Teign River. The Michelin-starred restaurant is renowned for creating innovative European dishes using superb Devon produce and features an impressive wine cellar to match the high standard of cooking. £££
Sandy Park Inn
tel: 01647-432 114; www.sandyparkinn.co.uk; food served Mon–Sat 6–8.30pm.
Enjoy good unpretentious home-made food and a friendly welcome at this thatched 17th-century inn near Castle Drogo, which can be seen from the terrace. ££

Have your photo taken with a friend.

Tour 7

North Devon

Discover North Devon's popular resorts of Woolacombe and Ilfracombe, then continue westwards to charming Clovelly and the wild coast off Hartland Point.

This 77-mile (124km) tour will take you a full day if you are driving, more if you want to make the most of all the attractions en route.

BRAUNTON

Our journey begins at **Braunton ❶**, where surf shops give a clue of what is to come and the Museum of British Surfing (Caen Street; tel: 01271-815 155; www.museumofbritishsurfing. org.uk; Apr–Dec Tue–Sun 11am–3pm, Mar Sat & Sun only) charts the history of surfing and displays memorabilia. The flat land nearby is more interesting than it seems; what used to be RAF Chivenor is now a base for the Royal Marines, and beyond it is the Braunton Great Field, an ancient field system with divisions still visible.

Highlights

- Woolacombe Beach
- Ilfracombe
- Wildlife and Dinosaur Park
- Barnstaple Pannier Market
- Westward Ho!
- Clovelly
- Hartland Quay and Point

Wander down these lanes to **Braunton Burrows** – sand dunes known for their botany and birdlife – with views over the estuary. The whole area has been designated by Unesco as Britain's first Biosphere Reserve, because of its variety of habitats. Most visitors continue on to **Saunton**, an impressive stretch of beach,

Tarka Line and Trail

Take a low-impact day out exploring Devon's rolling hills by train on the Tarka Line. Opened in 1854, it follows the river valleys of Taw and Yeo from Exeter to Barnstaple. Tarka the otter, in Henry Williamson's famous tale of the same name, travels the same route. From Barnstaple station you can rent a bike and cycle the Tarka Trail, a traffic-free cycle path (Tarka Trail Cycle Hire; www.tarkabikes.co.uk).

Take the Tarka Trail on the traffic-free cycle path.

popular with sand-yachts, wind- and wave-surfers, although with limited access due to the golf club stretching along its back.

The road then girdles the headland to **Croyde Bay**, with holiday camps and an attractive beach, popular with both families and surfers – Croyde Bay provides one of the best surfing destinations in the UK, with good waves for experienced surfers. Lifeguards patrol the beach in summer.

Take the right turn up through the pretty village and on via a narrow road to **Georgeham**, shoe-horned into a narrow valley. This is where Henry Williamson wrote *Tarka the Otter*.

From here, **Woolacombe** ❷, the finest beach in Devon, is tantalisingly close. Turn left, and the road descends gradually to the beach below. The beauty of Woolacombe is the uniform sand, the dunes and the green sward behind them. On non-beach days a fine alternative is to round the corner to Mortehoe, park the car and walk to **Morte Point** ❸, on a grassy headland with great cliff scenery.

ILFRACOMBE

The most important resort of the north is **Ilfracombe** ❹, although it lacks a beach of quality. A fishing village until the 19th century, its natural harbour brought steamer traffic and the railway. The tide of tourism rose quickly, and the population had doubled by 1860, and doubled again by 1891. But the high watermark had been reached: the tide has since receded, leaving the town fossilised between then and now.

Ilfracombe's location is a good one, and its unprepossessing main street up the hill away from the main tourism area, preserving the holiday enclave to which three small shoreline hills provide shelter. The most seaward (Lantern Hill) protects the characterful **port.** Lundy trips, sea fishing charters and seasonal coastal cruises aboard a paddle-steamer are offered here. Lantern Hill is crowned by **St Nicholas Chapel**, with neat whitewashed interior and all-round view.

Braunton Burrows.

At the foot of the third shoreline hill you'll reach the eccentric **Museum** (www.ilfracombemuseum. co.uk; Apr–Oct Mon–Sat 10am–5pm, Nov–Mar Tue–Fri 10am–1pm). The collection charts the resort's heyday and includes plenty of oddities: a collection of pickled bats, a two-headed kitten, and the Ilfracombe radio station.

The road east out of Ilfracombe rolls around the coast. It plunges down to sea level at **Watermouth Cove**, with its natural harbour. Watermouth Castle has been converted

Woolacombe has won awards for having the best beach in Britain.

Ilfracombe, North Devon's principal resort, is in an incomparable setting.

into a family theme park (www.water mouthcastle.com).

COMBE MARTIN

Combe Martin ❺ is not much more than a one-street town, but the street runs some 2 miles (3km) from the head of the valley to the sea. At the top of the valley is the **Wild-life and Dinosaur Park** ❻ (tel: 01271-882 486; www.cmwdp.co.uk; Feb half term–Oct daily 10am–5pm), one of the premier attractions in the region, with full-size dinosaur models in the woods, a Dino Express train ride, a playzone area, plus wildlife including sea lions, lions, penguins and meerkats.

Combe Martin's most unusual building is the **Pack of Cards** pub, built by a gambler to resemble just that, with 52 windows and 52 doors.

On the far side of the bay, Little Hangman rises steeply out of the sea. There are fine walks up to its peak from the car park, and thence onto the shoulder of Great Hangman.

The A399 climbs inland from the town onto the fringes of Exmoor. Off to the right is **Arlington Court** ❼ (NT; tel: 01271-850 296; mid-Feb–Oct daily 11am–4/5pm, weekends

Nov–mid Dec), North Devon's only substantial country house open to the public. Built in 1822, it has a large carriage museum, and is imprinted with the character of its most recent owner, Rosalie Chichester, a grand dame and collector. Its superb parkland includes a heronry.

Also worth a detour, on the other side of the A399, is the tiny church of **St Petrock** ❽, on the upper edge of the nestled village of **Par-**

Playtime in Ilfracombe

Parents with kids in tow will enjoy Ilfracombe's Tunnels Beaches complex (www.tunnelsbeaches. co.uk; Apr–Oct daily 10am–6pm, check the website for early closing times). It is a short walk through the caves, which display some interesting facts and figures. Sit back and admire the lovely rugged scenery while kids play safely in the tidal pool, skim stones and explore the rock pools. The shop overlooking Ladies' beach sells souvenirs and there is a small café. Gentlemen's beach is shut off when there is a wedding taking place.

The stunning garden and conservatory at Arlington Court.

racombe. Parts of this church may be 13th century, but because it was supplanted by a newer church, it remains a relic of the 18th century, with hand-lettered scriptures on the screen, rickety pews and planking. Instructions for obtaining the key can be found at the church.

The A399 skirts the edge of the moor, with fine views off to the left, past **Exmoor Zoo** (www.exmoorzoo.co.uk; daily 10am–5pm, till 6pm June–mid-Sept, dusk in winter), before dipping down into the lush Bray valley and thence to **South Molton**, a pleasant Georgian market town known for its antiques shopping. From here it's a 12-mile (20km) drive to Barnstaple on the A361.

BARNSTAPLE

Barnstaple ❾ is a farming town where industrial estates and shopping centres have bloomed in the past decade. The town has a long history. Pilton, a district to the west of the centre, received its royal charter in 930, making it one of the oldest burghs in England. Early success was due to Barnstaple's position at the highest navigable and lowest crossable point of the River Taw, but silting up and the growth of Bideford put paid to serious trade.

Little remains of Barnstaple's origins. The Norman Castle, near the Civic Centre, is just a mound spiked with trees. The first bridge was built in 1273, and although it has been much altered since, you can still see the original brickwork if you take

The Albert Memorial Clock in Barnstaple town square.

Meerkat at Exmoor Zoo.

the riverside underpass at the east end. The town's strategic position was highlighted again at the beginning of the railway age when five lines converged here, of which only one remains. More recently, the arrival of the A361 link road brought another resurgence.

Penetrate through a narrow lane halfway down Butcher's Row near the **Pannier Market** and you enter a hidden, grassy square with the unexceptional St Peter's Church to the right and the graceful **St Anne's Chapel** (1330) in the centre. The chapel has had many functions, and once housed the grammar school attended by poet John Gay.

The centre of town rather ignores Barnstaple's square, with its Albert Memorial Clock, but don't miss the **Museum** (Mon–Sat 10am–5pm, closes 4pm winter; free), next to the bridge. Hands-on displays highlight wildlife, sea life, transport, industry and folklore of the area in an excellent, compact collection.

Just down river from the square is the colonnaded **Queen Anne's Walk** (1709), where merchants gathered to do their deals with the figure of the Queen above their heads. Upriver from the square, up Litchdon Street, you can admire the **Penrose Almshouses** (1627); linger within the quad and one of the residents might just give you a tour.

BIDEFORD

Continue out on the Bideford road, which eventually leaves the Taw estuary and swings left to meet the Torridge. Across the water are views of first Appledore, with its covered shipyard, and then **Bid-**

Barnstaple Pannier Market

A focal point of Barnstaple is the Pannier Market (tel: 01271-379 084; Mon–Sat 9am–4pm), housed in an 1855 building on the High Street. This is the best of Devon's many such markets, offering a wide range of fresh produce, handmade arts and crafts together with antiques and collectables. Organic fruit and vegetables are also on sale throughout the week in Butcher's Row, a colourful parade of shops that runs along the market flank.

Inside the Barnstaple Pannier Market.

Bideford Quay, once the hub for imports of tobacco, wool and timber.

eford **⑩** itself, with a jumble of houses and shops behind a pretty riverside quay.

The link-road bridge, high overhead, has released the pressure on Bideford's 24-arch bridge, much of which dates from 1535, but the quay remains the focus of town life. Bideford was once the third-largest port in Devon, and ships left here for the Americas, although shallow waters restricted significant later development. Today, most of the space is taken by fishing boats and leisure craft.

At the far end of the Bideford quay is Victoria Park, and the **Burton Art Gallery and Museum** (www.burtonartgallery.co.uk; Mon–Sat 10am–4pm, Sun 11am–4pm; free), an arts space of great distinction and great aspirations, with a small museum up-

Lundy Island

Lundy Island is a lonely, peaceful 3-mile (5km) slice of high land 11 miles (18km) offshore where puffins well outnumber the resident population. Owned by the National Trust and managed by the Landmark Trust, Lundy is rich in curiosities and natural history. Activities include diving, climbing, birdwatching, fishing and snorkelling. There's a pub and restaurant, shop and a variety of accommodation (including the old lighthouse). The MS *Oldenburg* sails to Lundy from Bideford and Ilfracombe (Apr–Oct). For more information, tel: 01271-863 636; www.landmarktrust.org.uk/Lundyisland.

A Lundy puffin: the island's most iconic bird.

stairs and an education centre. The quay is also the mainland station for **Lundy Island**.

Appledore is still fundamentally a fishing and boat-building village, with close-packed white cottages climbing the hill, and a small seasonal **maritime museum** (www.northdevon maritimemuseum.co.uk) up above, from where there are tremendous estuary views.

Around the corner facing the open sea is the Victorian resort town of **Westward Ho!** ⓫, its name borrowed from the epic novel by Charles Kingsley which is based on Bideford, home to Kingsley in the 1850s. The resort was created by a 19th-century development company who realised the potential of the 2 miles (3km) of sandy beach and extensive grasslands of Northam Burrows.

One of the most innovative of Devon's farm attractions is **The Big Sheep** ⓬ (tel: 01237-472 366; www.thebigsheep.co.uk; Apr–Oct daily 10am–6pm, limited winter opening) at Abbotsham, just off the A39. Anything to do with sheep takes place here – lamb-feeding, shearing, sheep-dog trials and even sheep racing – plus rides and attractions.

CHARMING CLOVELLY

The A39 shadows the coast to just above **Clovelly** ⓭ (tel: 01237-431 781; www.clovelly.co.uk; summer 9am–6pm, shorter hours in winter), a perfectly preserved fishing village that flows like spilt paint down a steep hill to a small harbour.

The whole village is owned by the Clovelly Estate, purchased in 1738 by the Hamlyn family, who still live in Clovelly Court at the top of the hill. There is a visitor centre by the car park at the entrance to Clovelly, and below it the village is remarkably unspoiled, with bumpy cobbles to negotiate in the walk down to the fishing cove (a Land-Rover service operates in season however).

Most of the village's income is derived from its 300,000 or so annual visitors, although fishing boats do still function. Charles Kingsley lived here (see page 36), while his father was curate at the church, and a small Kingsley museum is adjacent to a preserved fisherman's cottage. The Clovelly lifeboat is still active

The Burton Art Gallery and Museum also contains a Tourist Information Centre.

and the lifeboat house is often open to the public in summer.

HARTLAND POINT

This is undoubtedly a treacherous coast for ships, and nowhere more so than off **Hartland Point** ⓮, the last stop on this route. This is Devon's coast at its most wild.

Hartland's layout has been determined by the weather. Its lighthouse is right on the point, while the village, with a long, low main street, is a couple of miles inland. The manorial residence of **Hartland Abbey** (tel: 01237-441 496; www. hartlandabbey.com; Apr–Sept Sun–Thu 2–5pm, gardens 11am–5pm) is tucked into a sheltered valley below the village of Stoke, on the way to Hartland Quay. The abbey remains date from 1157 and the main house from 1779. The Stucley family, who still own Hartland Abbey, have their own side chapel in **St Nectan's church** up above, which has the tallest tower (128ft/38m) in North Devon. Note the counterweighted church gate.

From here it is a short descent to **Hartland Quay,** which today is lit-

Down the cobbled lanes of Clovelly through traditional whitewashed cottages.

tle more than a hotel clinging to some of the finest cliff scenery in Britain. The quay was authorised by an act of Parliament back in 1586, and it was still functioning at the end of the 19th century, since when storms have smashed it to smithereens. This is a strikingly beautiful place, backed by massive cliffs with muscular veined strata, and likely to leave a lasting impression on the visitor who comes here on a stormy day.

Clovelly harbour at low tide.

Head to Hartland Point for glorious walking and dramatic coastal views along the South West Coast Path.

Eating Out

Croyde
The Thatch
14 Hobbs Hill; tel: 01271-890 349; www.thethatchcroyde.com; daily breakfast, lunch and dinner.
Surfing dudes and sea dogs mingle merrily at this cob barn pub. Eats include steaks, burgers, nachos and jacket potatoes. ££

Woolacombe
nc@ex34
South Street; tel: 01271-871 187; www.noelcorston.com; daily Thu–Sat at 7pm, booking essential.
Come here for that special occasion where chef Noel Corston produces a fixed multi-course tasting menu built around the seasons. £££

Ilfracombe
Thomas Carr @ The Olive Room
56 Fore Street; tel: 01271-867 831; www.thomascarrdining.co.uk; Wed–Sat dinner, Fri–Sat lunch also.
Set in a 19th-century townhouse, this talented local chef delivers creative distinct flavours in unpretentious surroundings, which has gained the restaurant a Michelin-star. £££

Barnstaple
Alfie Browns
55 Boutport Street; tel: 01271-344 477; www.alfiebrowns.co.uk; daily lunch and dinner.
You'll find the full range, from sandwiches and tapas to pies and steaks at this modern take on the traditional pub. ££

Bideford
Hoops Inn
Horns Cross, Nr Clovelly; tel: 01237-451 222; www.hoopsinn.co.uk; daily lunch and dinner.
Long, low thatched pub on the A39 between Bideford and Clovelly, featuring real ale and fish fresh from the North Devon coast.
££

Appledore
Market Street Kitchen
25 Market Street; tel: 01237- 474 168; www.marketstkitchen.com; daily 10am–4pm.
This pretty little tearoom is the perfect venue for high quality, homemade breakfasts, coffee, light lunches and afternoon tea. £

The magnificent coastline near Great Hangman.

Tour 8

Exmoor

Explore heather-covered moors and dramatic, beautiful coastline on this 67-mile (108km) full-day car and walking tour of Britain's second-smallest national park.

Exmoor National Park may be small at 265 sq miles (670 sq km) but it offers an incredible variety of landscapes and wildlife, with wild red deer and Exmoor ponies among its blanket bogs and valley woodlands. A quarter of the park is in Devon and the rest in Somerset, more extensively farmed than Dartmoor and with habitation more widespread. Its long history is charted in some Bronze Age remains: many hills are topped by Iron Age forts or Beaker period barrows, while Tarr Steps is finer than any 'clapper' bridge found on Dartmoor.

COMBE MARTIN

This tour begins from **Combe Martin ❶**, at the western edge of Exmoor. Be warned: the first section follows

Highlights

• Lynmouth Cliff Railway
• Doone Valley
• Selworthy
• Dunster
• Dunkery Beacon

the dramatic coastline through steep and difficult roads, of which the first is a taste of what's to come: Shute Lane leaves Combe Martin's main street just down from the Pack o' Cards pub see page 67 and rapidly climbs to such a height that Dartmoor can sometimes be seen on a clear day, to the south. On the left of the road is **Great Hangman ❷**, reached by footpath, with breathtaking clifftop scenery.

HOLDSTONE DOWN

After a couple of miles running parallel with the valley of Combe Martin, turn left at a junction signed to Trentishoe and Hunter's Inn. Shortly after the turning you'll pass the National Park sign. Here, too, the views continue, with the vale of Parracombe dropping down to the right, and the barren 1,146ft (344m) **Holdstone Down** with fine walking and cliff scenery rising up to the left.

The road then slips inland down into the thickly wooded Heddon Valley. At the bottom, the half-timbered **Hunter's Inn** is a popular refreshment stop and focal point for walks. Take the steep road alongside the inn signed to Martinhoe, and then go left towards Woody Bay at the next T junction. Following signs to Lynton, take the toll road up through the Lee Abbey estate. Looking down is the **Valley of the Rocks**, a dramatic land formation thought to have been created by the River Lyn.

LYNTON

The road climbs out of the valley and into the back of **Lynton** ❸, another Victorian development. George Newnes, publisher of the Sherlock

Enjoying the water in the Doone Valley.

Holmes stories, gave the town its grand Town Hall, where the tourist information office is located. Take a right down into Queen Street for the heart of the town. Round the corner at the bottom is the seasonal **Lyn and Exmoor Museum** (Easter–Oct Tue–Thu, Sat 10.30am–1.30pm, 2–5pm), in a cob cottage.

Lynmouth's ❹ main attraction is its location. Its small harbour is guarded by the Rhenish Tower. The **Cliff Railway** (see box) arrives on the seafront. Nearby on The Esplanade is an **Exmoor National Park Centre**, housed in the Lynmouth Pavilion, which includes a replica of the town's most famous lifeboat and hosts a varied events programme.

East from Lynmouth on the A39, **Watersmeet ❺**, a 19th-century fishing lodge turned into a tearoom and shop (National Trust), is a good place to start a walk, and from here you should head upstream. Walk up the East Lyn River and you'll emerge at Brendon, on the doorstep of the **Doone Valley ❻**. The actual story of R D Blackmore's *Lorna Doone* has become less well known than the region itself, dubbed Doone Country. Lorna and her hero John Ridd were married in **Oare Church**, where Blackmore's grandfather was vicar.

To travel to the valley by car, leave Lynmouth on the Porlock road up Countisbury Hill and once past County Gate (you are entering Somerset) take a right signed to Brendon. Turn left at the bottom for Malmsmead, and the pretty, winding valley climbs gradually into bandit country, marked by the attractive little **Robber's Bridge**. Return to the A39, and descend (the toll road has better views) to **Porlock**.

SELWORTHY

Picture-book prettiness lies a little further east, in **Selworthy ❼**. Lying at the heart of the National Trust's Holnicote estate, the village was rebuilt in 1828 by Sir Thomas Acland of

The Cliff Railway

Sherlock Holmes' publisher, George Newnes, financed the building of the Cliff Railway (tel: 01598-753 486; www.cliffrailwaylynton.co.uk; mid-Feb–mid-Nov daily 10am–5pm with exceptions) which links Lynton with Lynmouth, 500ft (150m) below. The railway is worked by water. The car at the bottom discharges its 700 gallons until the weight of the top car is sufficient to pull it to the top, the most environmentally friendly way to travel. You can enjoy a beer, a snack and the awesome view at the Cliff Top Café.

Killerton, who used traditional designs and materials to create a deliberately old-fashioned village of cream-washed stone thatched cottages to house the aged and infirm of the estate. Continue on to **Dunster ❽**, a well-preserved medieval town with a dramatic 19th-century **Castle** (Mar–Oct daily 11am–5pm) and 17th-century circular **Yarn Market**.

Our route turns inland, up the A396. After some miles turn right at Wheddon Cross, towards Exford. If the day is clear, branch right to Dunkery Beacon, Exmoor's highest spot at 1,705ft

Tarr Steps across the River Barle has been here for around 3,000 years.

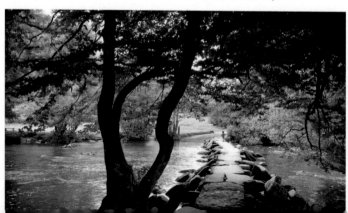

(519m). The Beacon rises gradually, the walk is easy, and from the top one can supposedly see 16 counties.

EXFORD

Exford ❾, sheltering in the Exe valley, is the heart of Exmoor and the centre for Exmoor recreation.

Cross the river bridge and turn left up the hill. At the top, go straight over the crossroads, through a ford to **Landacre Bridge**. Cross Landacre, climb out of the valley and turn left to **Withypool**. Follow the signs for **Tarr Steps** ❿. Descend to the car park and walk down to this 17-span 'clapper' bridge, said to be up to 3,000 years old.

Back up on Winsford Hill, retrace your steps a mile or so and take a right down into the pretty village of **Wins-**

Water-powered cable car.

ford, dominated by the Royal Oak Inn. The A396 runs to the east of Winsford. Head south, and turn off it at the signpost for **Dulverton.** This handsome farming town on the River Barle is where our Devonian journey ends.

Eating Out

Combe Martin
Pack o' Cards Inn
High Street; tel: 01271-882 300; www.packocards.co.uk; Mon–Sat lunch and dinner, Sunday noon–8pm.
Constructed to look like a deck of cards, this pub spans four floors. There's a good range of light lunches and full-restaurant meals, plus a Sunday carvery. £

Lynton
The Rockford Inn
Brendon; tel: 01598-741 214; www.therockfordinn.co.uk; daily lunch and dinner, closed Mon for food in winter, open for drinks from 6pm.
Take a pew by the river and enjoy real ale along with game pie or a bowl of River Exe mussels. Popular with local farmers, fishermen and ramblers. ££

Lynmouth
The Rising Sun
Harbourside; tel: 01598-753 223; www.risingsunlynmouth.co.uk; daily lunch and dinner. ££

Loved locally for its high standards, its simple menu draws on local game and seafood. RD Blackmore wrote some of *Lorna Doone* here; the poet Shelley is believed to have honeymooned here and Coleridge once stayed too. £££

Porlock
Locanda on the Weir
Porlock Weir; tel: 01643-863 300; www.locandaontheweir.co.uk; food served Wed–Sun noon–8pm.
Classic Italian cuisine is created using the best of local Exmoor produce at this classy restaurant overlooking Porlock Weir. £££

Dulverton
Tarr Farm
Tarr Steps; tel: 01643-851 507; www.tarrfarm.co.uk; daily breakfast, lunch, afternoon tea and dinner.
A converted 16th-century farm, next to the ancient 'clapper', is now a traditional inn committed to using local suppliers. ££

The quays of East Looe are lined with trawlers.

Tour 9

The South Coast Harbours and Bodmin Moor

This 74-mile (120km) tour explores the pretty south coast harbours – Looe, Polperro, Polruan and Fowey – then heads inland to Bodmin Moor and the extraordinary Eden Project.

This tour encompasses many of Cornwall's gems and should ideally be done over a couple of days – if not three – to give them the time and attention they deserve. Look at our Accommodation pages (see page 124) for our recommendations in the area.

LISKEARD

Liskeard ❶ (on the A38 from Saltash) still has much to offer in the wealth of its Georgian buildings, second only to Truro. **St Martin's** is a plain, no-nonsense church; the Victorian **Guildhall** is Italianate in style and includes a clock tower. There are imposing stone and slate-hung houses in

Highlights

- Liskeard
- East Looe
- Polperro
- Fowey
- Bodmin Moor
- Lanhydrock
- Eden Project
- Lost Gardens of Heligan

The Parade, a Regency **Market Hall**, and Stuart House, where Charles I slept for nine nights during the Civil War (1642–6), and now housing an arts and heritage centre. The Liskeard & District Museum (Mon–Fri 10am–

Tourism money is vital to East Looe's prosperity.

4pm, Sat 10am–1pm; free) on Pike Street tells the story of the town's mining and agricultural industries, and its social history. Well Lane has a surprise attraction – although it looks as if it wants to keep it hidden: in an arched grotto, water, once believed to have curative properties, spouts from the 16th-century **Pipe Well**.

Unexpected pleasures

Take the B3254 south, which hugs the railway and the old Liskeard–Looe Canal as far as St Keyne Station.

A lane opposite climbs up to **St Keyne's Well**, famous for giving a person who drank from it mastery over their spouse in marriage. Join the A387 and continue south to Looe.

EAST AND WEST LOOE

A deeply wooded valley joins that of the West Looe River, above the bridge that links East and West Looe, which were both given charters in the 13th century. **East Looe ②** is the larger and more commercially important; although its glory has faded, it's an attractive little town. The quays from which ore was loaded onto schooners now throng with visitors,

and warehouses have been converted into holiday flats, restaurants and shops. The town's prosperity depends on tourism and on a revival of the fishing industry, whose trawlers line the quay. The 15th-century **Old Guildhall** (mid-April–Oct daily 11am–4pm, Sat until 1.30pm) houses a museum devoted to mostly fishing and smuggling.

Across the bridge in **West Looe**, the 14th-century **Church of St Nicholas** on the quay has had a chequered career as a guildhall, prison and school. The **Jolly Sailor Inn** looks well adapted to its smuggling history.

POLPERRO

The drive to **Polperro ③** along the A387 is short and scenic. Polperro lives up to its reputation as Cornwall's most picturesque fishing village and though it never produced a recognised artists' colony, thousands of amateur artists come here to paint. Colour-washed cottages, some more than 300 years old, crowd the steep hillsides, converging on a brook that

Fowey from Polruan

Polruan lives on its magnificent views from the pretty cottages above the tiny harbour and passenger ferry. Because of a threat from French marauders in 1457, it has a blockhouse built on the rocks at the shore, the twin of one at Fowey. **Hall Walk**, with panoramic views of Fowey, is reached from Pont Pill Creek and follows the hillside. It is especially stunning in March and April when the daffodils carpeting the river banks are in bloom.

The waterside blockhouse and harbour at Polruan.

flows fast through the village, under stone bridges into the tiny harbour. Here, the **House on Props**, a 16th-century inn, is poised over the Roman – some say Saxon – bridge.

Cars are banished to the car park near Crumplehorn Mill Inn at the entrance to the village. Trams styled from converted milk floats take visitors to the top of the village. The Polperro-in-miniature **Model Village and Railway** (tel: 01503-272 378; www.polperromodelvillage.com; Easter–Oct daily 10.30am–6pm) is a popular attraction.

The **Heritage Museum of Smuggling and Fishing** (tel: 01503 273 005; Easter–Oct daily 10am–5pm) sits on the quayside, and brings to life Polperro's history through photographs and memorabilia. Take a path up the hillside to enjoy the splendid views.

POLRUAN AND THE FERRY

Polruan ❹ is Fowey's poor relation, declining as the town across the estuary prospered. From here follow the signs to **Bodinnick Ferry**, where car ferries make the two-minute crossing to Fowey at frequent intervals. 'Ferryside', on the waterfront, was once the

home of novelist Daphne du Maurier, the author of *Rebecca* and *Jamaica Inn*.

FOWEY

Houses huddle daintily around the deep-water harbour at **Fowey** ❺ (pronounced *Foy*), which calls itself 'Du Maurier Country' and has the **Du Maurier Literary Centre** on South Street which can be visited (tel: 01726-833 616; daily 10am–4.30pm; free). The Fowey estuary is one of the south coast's best sailing areas, but also has romantic creeks for landlubbers to explore, along with some upmarket little shops and galleries.

In Trafalgar Square, the little **Fowey Museum** (Easter–Sept Mon–Fri 10.30am–4.30pm) has a history of its very own: built in 1792, it incorporates a 14th-century chapel, did time as a prison and now charts Fowey's maritime past.

POLRIDMOUTH COVE AND MENABILLY

Polridmouth Cove ❻ (pronounced *Pridmouth*) can be reached from the Fowey–St Austell road and a small car park. A short walk downhill will take you to the cove and a landlocked pool below the woods of **Menabilly**. To this place of haunted beauty Daphne du Maurier came in 1943, leaving reluctantly 24 years later when her husband died and the owner refused to renew her lease.

LOSTWITHIEL

It's difficult now to believe that **Lostwithiel** ❼ (reached via the B3269 from Fowey, or the faster A390) was once Cornwall's capital, the centre of the tin industry and a flourishing port. Yet its historic presence is still there, half-hidden in this serene, French-looking place beside the River Fowey.

In Quay Street are the remains of Stannary Court, the 14th-century **Duchy Palace**, which served as the Hall of the Exchequer, Shire Hall and prison. There are also numerous attractive 18th-century buildings, including in Fore Street the former **Corn Exchange**. It houses the Lostwithiel Museum (www.lostwithielmuseum. org; Apr–Sept Mon–Fri 10.30am– 4.30pm; free), which evokes life during the 18th and 19th centuries.

Fowey History

Fowey had its time of glory seven centuries ago. When London could muster only 25 ships for the Siege of Calais in the Hundred Years' War, Fowey sent 47 ships and 700 men. Given a taste for action, these 'Fowey Gallants' turned pirates and carried on fighting even when the war was over. On one of their forays the French were unable to take **Place House**, the seat of the Treffry family, having failed to take account of the feisty resistance of Dame Elizabeth Treffry; although her husband was away fighting in the wars, she took them on and forced them to beat a hasty retreat. Today, the fairy-tale turrets and battlements of the largely 19th-century house provide the town with a peaceful and romantic backdrop.

Next stop is the 13th-century **Restormel Castle** ❽ (tel: 01208-872 687; www.english-heritage.org.uk; Apr–Oct daily 10am–4pm, with ex-

Polperro lives up to its reputation and paths winding up the hill offer splendid views over the picturesque harbour.

The manicured, landscaped Lanhydrock parkland.

ceptions). The circular keep over the artificially steepened hill and a deep moat (now dry) was regarded as a perfect military solution.

GATEWAY TO THE MOOR

Bodmin ❾, gateway to the Moor, is reached via the A30 from Launceston or Truro, or the B3268 from Lostwithiel. It was on the old trade route from Ireland to the continent, and attracted 5th-century Christians who often broke their lengthy journeys here.

Guron was the first, as evidenced by his holy well in St Petroc's churchyard and a roadside fountain. St Petroc, Cornwall's senior saint, followed in the 6th century, founding a priory of which only fragments remain. The 15th-century **Church of St Petroc** (daily 9am–5pm; free) has an important treasure: the casket that contained his relics. It has twice been stolen and returned, although without its contents. St Petroc's is Cornwall's largest church and its beautiful Norman font, supported by angels, is probably the best in the county. The church has good acoustics and is used as a venue for concerts.

Exploring the town

This sensible, hardworking town lost much of its administrative importance when its county town status was lost to Truro. The imposing, 19th-century **Shire Hall** (housing a helpful tourist office and the Courtroom Experience attraction) stands in Mount Folly Square. The Tudor guildhall next door is now **Bodmin Museum** (tel: 01208-77067; Apr–Sept Mon–Fri 10.30am–4.30pm, Sat 10.30–2.30pm; free); it contains a Cornish kitchen and a World War I display with a periscope to see and hear what life in trenches was like.

Some of the nation's most precious possessions, such as the Domesday Book (1086) and the crown jewels, were kept for safety during World War I in **Bodmin Jail** (tel: 01208-76292; www.bodminjail.org; daily 9.30am–8pm (until 6pm Oct–Mar); 'paranormal tours' every Friday and Saturday at 6.30pm. Public executions were held here in the middle of the 19th century; you can visit the dungeons for more gruesome details.

The town's close links with the Cornish Infantry regiment are il-

Restormel Castle.

lustrated in the **Regimental Museum** (www.cornwalls-regimental museum.org; mid-Mar–mid-Nov Tue–Sat 10am–5pm, mid-Nov–mid-Mar Wed–Sat 10am–4.30pm, Sun noon–4.30pm) in The Keep on the Lostwithiel Road.

Almost opposite is the station of the **Bodmin and Wenford Steam Railway** (tel: 01208-73555; www.bodminrailway.co.uk; May–Sept, check for train times and special events). It has a refreshment room and souvenir shop and offers special

events, as well as a nostalgic 6-mile (9km) trip.

LANHYDROCK

Bodmin's bypass (to the south) skirts the impressive 30-acre (12-hectare) parkland of **Lanhydrock ❿** (NT; tel: 01208-265 950; Apr–Sept Tue–Sun 11am–5.30pm, Mar and Oct until 5pm, with exceptions; park all year, daily). The Robartes family lived here for more than 300 years, and the National Trust has managed to retain a lived-in atmosphere.

THE MOOR

Travel eastwards on the A38 then north on a minor road to reach **Bodmin Moor ⓫**. This is a place to be treated with respect. Covering Cornwall's backbone in a granite blanket, it was home and shelter to the county's earliest inhabitants, and everywhere on the rock-strewn uplands are prehistoric stone circles, huts, barrows and medieval fields.

The bogs and heather of Bodmin Moor reach down the Loveny Valley to the road to Liskeard and **Carnglaze Slate Caverns** (tel: 01579-320 251; www.carnglaze.com; tours: Mon–Sat 10am–5pm,

Picnic Spot

The wooded valley above the bridges of Lostwithiel is commanded by 13th-century **Restormel Castle**. Fought over in the Civil War, it survives as an impressive ruin and the grounds make a delightful picnic spot and a place for children to play. Pick up some pasties from Fran's Pantry (1A Quay Street, Lostwithiel). And try some of their local cheeses: Yarg, Davidstow Cheddar, Cornish Organic Brie, a local Goat's Brie and Cornish Blue.

A place to spread out a rug and open a picnic hamper.

Vestiges of the tin industry on Bodmin Moor.

Aug until 8pm), with the most beautiful pool hidden in its depths.

St Neot, higher up the valley, has royal connections. The saint was King Alfred's brother and his church is a wonder of light and colour; 15 windows shine with stained glass that is among the finest in England. At Doublebois, a road forks left to join the Fowey River at **Golitha Falls** in a National Nature Reserve and, passing **King Doniert's Stone** – with a Latin inscription to Dungarth, King of Cornwall – allows access to the **Siblyback Lake**. Here there are water sports and trout fishing (permits required). **Trethevy Quoit**, easily accessible nearby, is a magnificent example of a Neolithic tomb.

Still following the river upstream, **Dozmary Pool** lies to the left in the wildest part of the moor. In Alfred Lord Tennyson's poetic vision, it was here that King Arthur's sword was consigned to the waters after his death.

At Bolventor is **Jamaica Inn** ⑫, which does its best to live up to the character conferred on it by Daphne du Maurier's eponymous romantic novel. The slate-hung Georgian buildings look as if they could still harbour smugglers (see page 124 for accommodation details) and there is a small smugglers' museum attached (daily 8am–9pm).

LEAVING THE MOOR

To the right of the A30, as you leave the moor, is **Blisland**. The Norman church (John Betjeman's favourite), with a brilliantly coloured screen

The Cheesewring granite tors, perched above a quarry.

Poetic Dozmary Pool.

and barrel roof, sits beside the only village green in Cornwall, an inn, a manor house and some cottages. Bypassing Bodmin, take the A391 that plunges into the much-abused

Lunar Landscape

Approaching St Austell you will see the landscape has been transformed by the extraction of china clay, with stark white spoil heaps and water-filled pools giving it a lunar appearance. Not pretty, but the industry used to be a mainstay of the economy. A Plymouth chemist, William Cookworthy, discovered the clay near Helston in 1746. Its exceptional purity made it ideal for the production of porcelain and paper, and demand encouraged investment in the construction of ports at Par and Charlestown. **Wheal Martyn China Clay Museum** (tel: 01726-850 362; www.wheal-martyn.com; daily 10am–5pm with exceptions, in the 26-acre (10-hectare) China Clay Country Park at Carthew, 2 miles (3km) north of St Austell, includes a disused works and brings the industry vividly to life; also nature trails and outdoor exhibits.

landscape of china clay country (see box). At Bugle, a diversion can be made to **Roche Rock**, a granite outcrop capped with the 15th-century St Michael's Chapel and a hermit's cell below, reached by a ladder.

St Austell ⓭ is the area's main town. The town centre has been regenerated but the old quarter, the Market Hall and tower of Holy Trinity Church, offer good photo opportunities.

Elsewhere are some fine old buildings, such as the White Hart Hotel and the **St Austell Brewery Visitor Centre** in Trevarthian Road (www.staustellbrewery.co.uk; Mon–Sat 9am–5.30pm, last entry 4pm; for tours, tel: 01726-66022).

THE EDEN PROJECT

At Bodelva, signposted from the A391 before you reach St Austell, you'll find Cornwall's most spectacular and well-marketed attraction, the **Eden Project ⓮** (see page 78).

CHARLESTOWN

Take the A390 past St Austell and follow signs to the port of **Charlestown ⓯**, the brainchild of Charles

Disused clay works, China Clay Country Park.

As made famous by the novel.

Rashleigh of Menabilly. Dug out of the beach in the 1790s, it has a granite-lined entrance and was intended for the shipment of both copper and tin. Today it sometimes caters for film crews, including the popular TV series Poldark. An inn or two, terraces of granite Georgian houses, stores and fish cellars provide the setting, and the **Charlestown Shipwreck Centre** (tel: 01726-69897; www.shipwreckcharles town.com; Tue–Sat 11am–3pm;

Expect stunning flora at the Lost Gardens of Heligan.

children under 5 free) tells the history of the town on both land and sea.

THE LOST GARDENS OF HELIGAN

The B3273 towards Mevagissey takes you to another of Cornwall's greatest attractions (also by Tim Smit of the Eden Project), the award-winning **Lost Gardens of Heligan** ⑯ (tel: 01726-845 100; www.heligan.com; daily Apr–Sept 10am–6pm, Oct–Mar 10am–5pm). These Victorian gardens became completely overgrown after the house was converted into a military hospital during World War I, and decades of neglect were compounded by the Burns' Day storm of 1990. The grounds are now beautifully restored, with boardwalks through a subtropical area, lakes, wetlands and woodlands in the Lost Valley, and vegetables and exotic fruits in the walled garden. The estate is a haven for wildlife; check out the Insect Hotel and the bee observation hide. Note that there is little shelter if the weather is bad.

MEVAGISSEY

Pilchards were once the mainstay of **Mevagissey** ⑰, about a mile downhill from the Heligan turning. 'Mevagissey Ducks', as they were called, were salted in barrels to victual the Royal Navy, and supported a fishing fleet that both filled the large double harbour and in fed a flourishing community.

The little **Mevagissey Museum** (tel: 01726-843 568; www.mevagis seymuseum.co.uk; Easter–Oct daily 11am–4pm, 11am–5pm July and Aug; free), housed in an 18th-century boat yard on East Quay, has an interesting collection of old photos and marine artefacts.

Waiting for the fish to bite in Charlestown.

Eating Out

Looe
Talland Bay Hotel
Talland Bay; tel: 01503-272 667; www.tallandbayhotel.co.uk; daily lunch and dinner.
This award-winning country-house-style restaurant offers everything freshly made, from Cornish crab and hand-dived scallops to locally-raised lamb. Local fruits in season and artisan cheeses also feature. There's a Sunday lunch menu that's popular with the locals – always a good sign. £££

Polperro
Nelsons
The Saxon Bridge, Big Green; tel: 01503-272 366; Tue–Sun dinner.
Situated on the River Pol, Nelsons specialises in seafood, including lobster and crab, and also offers vegetarian and gluten-free menus. Bookings are essential in the restaurant. ££

Fowey
King of Prussia
3 Town Quay; tel: 01726-833 694; www.kingofprussiafowey.co.uk; daily lunch and dinner.
Choose from light bites for lunch to substantial mains such as slow-cooked pork belly, followed by sticky toffee pudding with Cornish clotted cream. ££

Bodmin
Woods Cafe
Cardinham Woods, off the A38; tel: 01208-78111; www.woodscafecornwall.co.uk; daily 10.30am-4.30pm.
Enticing menu champions homemade food featuring Cornwall's amazing produce; cakes and scones are baked every morning and perfect with a pot of Tregothnan tea. £

St Austell
The Heligan Kitchen
The Lost Gardens of Heligan, Pentewan; tel: 01726-845100; www.heligan.com; daily 9.30am–5.30pm, 4.30pm in winter.
Open to all, this award-winning café serves Cornish cream teas, and soups and salads that use produce from its Victorian restorative garden. £

The Eden Project

A global garden, an environmental educational tool, an art gallery, a playground and an adventure – the Eden Project is Cornwall's most popular attraction.

When music producer Tim Smit inaugurated his giant conservatories, the 'biomes', he, along with an influx of new industries and large investments, ushered in a new era in Cornwall's history.

GREEN TECHNOLOGY

'The decline of industry in the 19th century affected Cornwall in a profound way,' explains chief executive Smit. When mining died it created a melancholy mood. But because of Cornwall's historical links with industry it was ready to embrace new technology, particularly green technology. What blossomed turned out to be a dawning of a post-industrial revolution.

The project, a 35-acre (14-hectare) site in a disused clay pit, has transformed one of the few unattractive areas of Cornwall into a place everybody wants to visit. It is a vast global garden, incorporating huge, dome-shaped biomes that resemble a surreal space station made of bubble-wrap.

BIOMES AND BEYOND

In the **Rainforest Biome**, the world's largest greenhouse, full of tropical plants, there is much to be learned about the coffee, banana and spice in-

Eden Project's biomes – the world's largest.

dustries on mini plantations. Here, too is the popular canopy walkway.

Inside the giant **Mediterranean Biome**, which re-creates the landscapes of the Mediterranean, California and South Africa, and the outdoor gardens, the crops – from olives and grapes indoors to hemp and sunflowers outside – are flourishing. And various growing systems are illustrated with models.

It is a place with serious environmental ambitions and there's a strong emphasis on education. Environmental lectures are conducted in the biomes, and The Core education centre, based on the structure of a sunflower, is designed according to Fibonacci's sequence, one of nature's basic building blocks, using fully sustainable materials. The permanent exhibition, Invisible Worlds, explores worlds beyond human senses and how life is shaped.

Kids Zone

The landscape at Eden is engineered to encourage curious young minds to explore their creativity in a playful way, with specific features and attractions dotted about to attract children (and adults) of all ages.

Lizard Point.

Tour 10

Truro to the Lizard

This 84-mile (135km) drive starts in the cobbled streets of Truro, trips down the tiny lanes to Falmouth, then continues on to the untamed Lizard and Land's End.

TRURO

Truro ❶ is unquestionably a city, albeit a small one, but its aspirations are evident in the 1980s Crown Court building, by Eldred Evans and David Shalev who went on to design Tate St Ives. Added to this are a handful of restaurants, cafés, hip bars and imaginative shops in the centre.

The **Cathedral**, also in the centre of town, was begun in 1880, four years after the diocese of Truro was created. Opposite are the **Assembly Rooms**, although Truro's best building is only skin-deep: the 1772 interior no longer exists.

In nearby Boscawen Street, the **City Hall** houses the Hall for Cornwall (undergoing redevelopment, due to open 2020), a venue for con-

Highlights

- Trelissick Gardens
- Falmouth and the National Maritime Museum
- Glendurgan Garden
- Trebah Garden
- Kynance Cove

certs, theatre, dance and light entertainment. Opposite, the ancient Coinage Hall has a pizzeria on the ground floor and the idiosyncratic **Charlotte's Tea Rooms**, surrounded by rooms full of antiques, upstairs. Don't miss a cream tea in this delightful Victorian setting.

On the other side of Boscawen Street, the past is well documented

The arrival of the railway secured Truro's economy.

in the **Royal Cornwall Museum** (www.royalcornwallmuseum.org. uk; daily 10am–4.45pm; under 16s free) in River Street. Its collection of archaeology, social history and art works from the Newlyn and St Ives Schools makes it one of the best museums in Cornwall.

TOWARDS THE ROSELAND PENINSULA

From Truro, the tree-shaded riverside road down the left bank of the River Truro climbs to the Heron Inn and the hanging gardens of **Malpas ❷**, with enchanting views of river and creek and quiet anchorages, once active with shipbuilding.

To reach the Roseland Peninsula, backtrack to the A390, go north and turn off just after **Tresillian** on the A3078. The road goes through **Tregony**, a sea port until the 17th century when the River Fal silted up with mush from the tin mines and clay pits. A left turn leads to the miniature fishing cove of **Portloe** where a stream reaches the beach from beneath the Lugger Hotel.

ST MAWES

Back on the A3078, take the left fork as you approach **St Mawes ❸** and follow the coastal road, past villas with lush, Mediterranean-style gardens, to the harbour. Pretty cottages, some thatched, line the seafront to the perfectly preserved **St Mawes Castle** (tel: 01326-270 526; www. english-heritage.org.uk; daily Apr–June and Sept–Oct 10am–5pm, July–Aug 10am–6pm, Nov–Mar Sat–Sun 10am–4pm with exceptions). Built in 1543, it is the best preserved of Henry VIII's defensive forts.

Leaving the village, take a left turn to **St Just-in-Roseland** ❹, where the lych gate of the church frames what is possibly Cornwall's most beautiful view. Reflected in St Just Pool, the 13th-century church makes a pleasing composition.

TRELISSICK GARDEN

The road back to Tregony invites exploration of backwaters: **Ruan Lanihorne**, which once had riverside wharves; and **St Michael Penkevil**, where the church and estate cottages cluster round the gates of

The churchyard at St-Just-in-Roseland offers great views.

The old Coinage Hall in Truro now houses a pizzeria and a tearoom.

Tregothnan, seat of the Boscawens, Earls of Falmouth. However, we take a more direct route to Trelissick and Falmouth on the B3289 from St Just, and board the King Harry Ferry, which makes the short trip across the Fal at 20-minute intervals (tel: 01872-861 917; www.falriver.co.uk for details).

Trelissick House, Grecian-style with a columned portico, is private, but **Trelissick Garden** ❺ is open to the public (NT; tel: 01872-862 090; daily, mid-Feb–Oct 10.30am–5.30pm, Nov–mid-Feb 10.30am–4.30pm or dusk). Among the National Trust's finest in Cornwall, the garden covers 25 acres (10 hectares) and is famous for hydrangeas and camellias. There is a lovely woodland walk.

DEVORAN TO PENRYN

At **Devoran** ❻ on Restronguet Creek (B3289 from Trelissick, then turn left and follow the creek around) are the grass-covered wharves and converted stores of a ghost port. Once connected by tramline with the mining area of Redruth, exporting minerals and importing coal, it survives on the sheer beauty of its situation.

Unusual Gardens

Cornwall is known for its benevolent climate that suits many unusual plant species, and, with over 60 gardens to visit, it's easy to find examples. A trip from Tresillian, off the A390, takes you to Trewithen (tel: 01726-883 647; www.trewithengardens.co.uk; call for opening times). Here you'll see superb rhododendrons and more, with many of the plants propagated up for sale. In 2012, Trewithen was awarded International Camellia Garden of Excellence – one of only 30 gardens in the world.

Lower down the creek is thatched **Pandora Inn**, named after the vessel that brought back Captain Bligh after the mutiny on the *Bounty*. **Mylor**, open to the Carrick Roads creek, is excellent for yachting.

Round Trefusis Point, facing Falmouth, is **Flushing**, reputed to have England's mildest climate. It gained its name in the 17th century when Dutch engineers, working on Falmouth's quays, settled here; their influence can still be seen in the tall houses lining the creek-side High Street.

In the 13th century **Penryn** was a seat of religious learning, subsequently becoming a major port, which declined as Falmouth grew. The granite and slate-hung buildings now enjoy Conservation Area status.

FALMOUTH

Falmouth ❼ started as a twinkle in Sir Walter Raleigh's eye. In the late 16th century, he decided it would make a good harbour, found Sir John Killigrew, the local lord, very responsive, and the development of the village of Pennycomequick was decided. By 1663 it had become Falmouth.

Falmouth's importance grew with its 1661 Charter. The arrival of the railway in 1863 to serve the new docks heralded the town's development as a holiday resort. Between the beaches and the station, quiet roads

Trelissick Garden, famous for its hydrangeas and camellias, also houses the National Collection of photinias and azaras.

are lined with hotels, guesthouses, villas and gardens, the loveliest of which are **Gyllyngdune Gardens**. Signposted from the seafront, paths lead into a sunken area planted with exotic trees and shrubs.

There are 450 years of military history to be explored at **Pendennis Castle** (tel: 01326-316 594; www.english-heritage.org.uk; Apr–Oct daily 10am–5pm with exceptions, Nov–Mar Sat–Sun 10am–4pm). It takes in a Tudor gun deck, underground tunnels and a World War II observation post. Pendennis was built by Henry VIII to protect the estuary from the French – a threat that never materialised. Encircling the headland is **Castle Drive**, which must be the most scenic in the West Country (follow the brown 'Scenic Route' signs).

Falmouth's showcase Maritime Museum has a huge collection of boats.

The quays and the centre

In Arwenack Street, parallel to the sea, the **Custom House**, with imposing Greek Doric columns, fronts Custom House Quay, where pub tables stand beside a small fishing harbour. From here, and from **Prince of Wales Pier**, ferries cross to St Mawes and Flushing, and make extended trips to Trelissick and up the River Fal to Malpas and, if the tide's right, to Truro.

Continue along Arwenack Street, lined with shops and restaurants, past the church and up to **The Moor**, Falmouth's municipal heart. Above the library, **Falmouth Art Gallery** (www.falmouthartgallery.com; Mon–Sat 10am–5pm; free) has a permanent display of Victorian and Edwardian paintings and some good temporary

Pendennis Castle has wonderful views over the Fal estuary.

Falmouth was developed after Sir Walter Raleigh rightly decided it would make a good harbour.

exhibitions. Across The Moor, the 111 stone steps of Jacob's Ladder climb the hillside to a pub of the same name. Follow the harbour still further, instead of turning inland, and you will eventually come to the Yacht Marina.

The Maritime Museum

Falmouth is not a wealthy town, but it has undergone a revival with the redeveloped quayside site, **Discovery Quay**. The sophisticated **National Maritime Museum Cornwall** (www.nmmc.co.uk; daily 10am–5pm), dominating the waterfront, is a stunning structure, with a floor-to-ceiling glass viewing gallery. There are lots of hands-on displays, a huge collection of boats of all kinds, and a chance to see traditional boat builders at work – as well as changing exhibitions and fantastic views over the harbour and town from the 95ft (29m) tower.

To the southwest the Helford River almost detaches the Lizard from the rest of Cornwall. From its east coast estuary, this yachting-friendly river cuts through rich woodland and sends inviting creeks through villages. In dramatic contrast, the plateau stretching to Lizard Point, the southernmost part of England, has beauty of a different kind.

GLORIOUS GARDENS

Leaving Falmouth via the popular beach of Swanpool, the road to Mawnan Smith is joined to visit two more wonderful gardens. The first is **Glendurgan Garden** ❽ (NT; tel: 01326-252 020; mid-Feb–Oct Tue–Sun 10.30am–

Poldark Mine

At Wendron, on the B3297, 2 miles (3km) north of Helston, parents with older children can step back in time at the Poldark Mine (www.poldarkmine.org.uk; underground tours 11am and 1pm, additional times during summer; see website for opening days).

The mine was closed in 1820, but its working days and conditions have been re-created. Winston Graham's popular *Poldark* novels, set in the 19th-century Cornish mining communities, made the name familiar, and the mine has been used for several of the BBC Poldark TV series, the latest of which was shot in 2018.

Trebah garden is a jungle of delights heading down a ravine to the river.

Taking care of rescued seals at the National Seal Sanctuary.

5.30pm, also Mon in Aug). Rare, exotic and subtropical plants fill the south-facing slopes of this wooded valley. A fantastic and very photogenic laurel maze, planted in 1833, has been renewed. The views here are great too.

The neighbouring garden, **Trebah** ❾ (tel: 01326-252 200; www.trebahgarden.co.uk; daily 10am–5pm or dusk), was first planted in the 1840s in a steeply wooded ravine running down to the river. Hydrangeas, rhododendrons and magnolias provide colour, and palms, tree ferns and giant gunnera populate the exotic background.

OYSTERS AND SEALS

A creek is skirted to **Port Navas**, where the Duchy of Cornwall has an oyster farm. About 5 miles (8km) southeast, reached via minor country lanes, is the tiny village of **Gweek** at the head of the Helford River.

Gweek is home to the **Cornish Seal Sanctuary** (tel: 01326-221 361; www.sealsanctuary.co.uk; daily, times vary according to season), which offers a hilltop park. Daphne du Maurier's **Frenchman's Creek** is at the end of a road to Kestle nearby.

A minor southbound road (joining the B3293 for the last stretch) drops down on the B3294 to pretty little **Coverack ⑪**. Still with a fleet of working boats, the tiny fishing village with thatched, whitewashed cottages is delightful.

Back on the B3293, which climbs to the Goonhilly Downs, standing among the hut circles and burial mounds of prehistory, are the satellite-tracking dishes of **Goonhilly Earth Station ⑫**, once the largest in the world. The Visitor Centre inside was closed in 2010 but there are proposed plans to open it again in the future.

Now take the road that runs through serpentine rock country all the way to Kuggar. The picturesque route descends along a gorge beside a cascading stream.

the heartening spectacle of rescued seals and sea lions cared for and re-turned to the wild after convalescence.

Turn left over the bridge and left through **Mawgan**. Among the mon-uments in the church are those to the Vyvyans of **Trelowarren** situated in parkland above a long wooded valley.

HELFORD AND COVERACK

Signposted through Manaccan is **Helford ⑩**, which has banished cars to

GETTING TO THE POINT

A great number of the thatched cot-tages in **Cadgwith ⑬**, at the road's end, downhill from Ruan Minor, are built of the black and green mottled serpentine rock – which brings charac-ter to the coved area. Two tiny coves are separated by a rocky viewpoint, the

Wild Food Walks

Join a guided walk led by specialist Rachel Lambert and learn about the abundance of wild food and how to identify edible plants. The walks take place all year round in the Lizard, West Cornwall, and last 2 to 3 hours. Participants learn about the historical and medicinal uses of local plants. And along with foraging guidelines, you will acquire some tasty new recipes. Tel: 07903 412014; www. wildwalks-southwest.co.uk.

Learning to identify what's good to eat and what's not.

Todden. A pub and pilchard cellars (one now housing the Old Cellars restaurant) complete the picture. The A3083 runs straight down the peninsula to **Lizard**, England's most southerly village.

The **Lizard Lighthouse**, signposted from the village centre, was begun by Sir John Killigrew of Falmouth in 1619, but the present buildings date from 1752.

KYNANCE COVE

Leaving the A3083, you reach **Kynance Cove** ⑭ on the Lizard's west coast. It is an unforgettable sight at low tide, with the golden sands and the green, red and purple of the serpentine set against the Prussian blue of the sea. **Mullion Cove** has long defied fierce southwesterly gales but climate change and rising sea levels put its future at risk. To the north, before Poldhu Cove, an obelisk on the cliff records the transmission of the first wireless signals across the Atlantic, sent by Guglielmo Marconi in 1901.

FLAMBARDS VILLAGE AND HELSTON

Back to the A3083 and, as Helston is approached, you come to a re-created Victorian village in landscaped gardens at Culdrose Manor. This is **The Flambards Experience** ⑮ (tel: 01326-573 404; www.flambards. co.uk; Apr–Oct daily 10am–5pm with exceptions, see website for

There is a roller coaster and funfair at The Flambards Experience.

hours). A popular family day out, it includes a funfair with a log flume, the white-knuckle ride Sky Force, and roller coaster rides.

Helston ⑯ is a bustling market town that comes alive on 8 May when it celebrates Flora Day. In Old Butter Market, the **Helston Museum** (www.helstonmuseum.co.uk; Mon–Sat 10am–4pm; free) portrays West Cornish life past and present. Water runs down open conduits in Coinagehall Street past the 17th-century **Blue Anchor Inn**, distinguished by its thatched roof and by the quality of the home-brewed beer.

Loe Pool lies just south of Helston, right in the heart of the Penrose Estate. Both are in the care of the National Trust and there is a numerous choice of walking paths through the lovely countryside.

Wild flowers along the Lizard coastal walk.

Kynance Cove is a beautiful spot.

HIDDEN TREASURE

Northwest of Helston on the B3302, a left turn leads you to the beautiful Tudor **Godolphin House** (NT; tel: 01736-763 194; garden daily 10am–4/5pm). This romantic house (closed to the public) and garden have an air of antiquity and peace. The garden boasts an original medieval layout, and is considered to be one of the most important historic gardens in Europe.

Eating Out

Truro
Tabb's
85 Kenwynn Street; tel: 01872-262 110; www.tabbs.co.uk; Tue–Fri lunch and dinner, Sat dinner.
Carefully chosen, seasonal ingredients handled with respect by Chef Nigel Tabb, who keeps the customers happy with his simple dishes. £££

St Mawes
Café Chandlers
1 The Quay; tel: 01326-270 998; daily 8.30am–5pm.
In a perfect location overlooking the harbour, come here for breakfast, coffee, delicious cakes and pasties, and well-filled sandwiches. £

Mylor
Pandora Inn
Restronguet Creek; tel: 01326-372 678; www.pandorainn.com; food served daily 10.30am–9.30pm.
This slate-floored thatched inn has a great waterside setting. The emphasis is on Cornish produce, especially seafood, and there are cream teas in summer too. ££

Falmouth
The Cove
Maenporth Beach; tel: 01326-251 136; www.thecovemaenporth. co.uk; Tue–Sat lunch and dinner, Sun noon–4pm.
The dining room with retractable roof and sliding glass doors offers true al-fresco dining and uninterrupted views across Falmouth Bay. Dishes are based on quality, seasonal produce found right on the doorstep. ££

Porthleven (nr Helston)
Kota
The Harbour Head; tel: 01326-562 407; www.kotarestaurant.co.uk; Tue–Sat dinner, closed Jan–mid-Feb.
"Kota" is Maori for shellfish, and the restaurant is renowned for its stunning seafood with a light Asian twist. £££

Tour 11

Land's End Peninsula and St Ives to St Agnes

This full-day, 65-mile (104km) car tour covers the dramatic tip of the Cornish peninsula before heading inland towards Camborne and Redruth.

PENZANCE

Sunny, south-facing **Penzance** ❶ is superbly situated in the embrace of Mount's Bay, where the grandeur of St Michael's Mount provides a focal point. This is one of the warmest places in Britain, with frost and snow almost non-existent. The gateway to the Land's End Peninsula, it has air and sea services to the wonderful Isles of Scilly (see page 108).

Historical background

Mentioned in the Domesday Book and granted a weekly market by Edward III, Penzance first claimed attention in 1595 when Spanish galleons appeared in the bay and the nearby villages of Paul, Mousehole and Newlyn were sacked and burned. It was also fair game for pirates during the 17th and 18th centuries. Charles II gave it the privilege of coining tin, but only in Victorian times did it assume its present character.

Highlights

- Penzance
- St Michael's Mount
- Mousehole
- Minack Theatre
- St Ives, the Tate and Barbara Hepworth Museum
- St Agnes

The flamboyant Egyptian House in Penzance.

Touring the town

From the east, past the station and inland from the large Wharfside Shopping Centre opposite the harbour, the main thoroughfare, **Market Jew Street**, climbs to the town centre and the grandiose, granite Market House (1836). A statue of Sir Humphry Davy, born nearby in 1778, tempts seagulls. The hand of his statue rests on the miners' safety lamp that bears his name.

There are handsome 18th- and early 19th-century buildings in **Chapel Street**, which runs left from the Market House, many with a ghostly story to tell as Chapel Street is Penzance's oldest street. Today a number of restaurants and art galleries occupy premises here. In Princes Street, The Exchange (www.newlynartgallery.co.uk; Mon–Sat 10am–5pm, closed Mon in winter) is a stunning art gallery with an undulating glass facade. The **Egyptian House**, a vividly coloured exercise in Egyptian style, was built in 1838. Further down the street, **St Mary's Church** commands the harbour from a peaceful graveyard.

Cornish painters

Close by are Morrab Gardens where subtropical plants flourish. Wander through and you emerge in Morrab Road, a quiet street lined with guesthouses. At the far end is Penlee Park with a walled memorial garden and the stylish Penlee House Gallery and Museum (www.penleehouse.org.uk;

Penzance's seawater lido is perfect on a summer's day

Mon–Sat, Apr–Oct 10am–5pm, Nov–Mar until 4.30pm, under 18s free). It is well worth a visit to see many of the works of the Newlyn School painters.

Back on the seafront, a left turn along the broad promenade takes you to the Art Deco Jubilee Pool, designed in 1930.

ST MICHAEL'S MOUNT

East of Penzance, the rocky island of **St Michael's Mount ➋** looms across the bay and, inevitably, comparison is made with the Mont-St-Michel in Normandy. The connection is more than a visual one: England's Edward the Confessor gave the island to the Benedictine monks of St-Michel and by 1140 they had founded a church there.

Newlyn Art Gallery.

The castle (NT; tel: 01736-710 265; www.stmichaelsmount. co.uk; Apr–Oct Sun–Fri 10.30am–5/5.30pm, all visits depend on weather conditions) crowns the Mount, which is reached by a cobbled causeway at low tide or by ferry when the tide is high.

Marazion ➌, at the terrestrial end of the causeway, was granted an early charter, in 1257. It became an important market town: the pronunciation of Maghas Yow – Thursday Market – has blurred over the years to Marazion. Located on the first floor of the Town Hall (the former fire station) is the **Town Museum** (May–Oct Mon–Fri 10.30am–4.30pm); the back section was once the town gaol and a reconstructed police cell can be viewed.

DETOUR TO TRENGWAINTON GARDEN

From St Michael's Mount, take the A30 west, turn right to Heamoor then west to **Trengwainton Garden ➍** (NT; tel: 01736-363 148; mid-Feb–Oct Sun–Thu 10.30am–5pm). In five intimate walled gardens, semitropical and tender plants not found elsewhere in mainland Britain are grown outdoors. Views over Mount's Bay are shared with **Madron**. Here, in St Maddern's Church, the Trafalgar Banner commemorates news of Nelson's death.

Ancient Relics

By turning right at Morvah, just past the Geevor Tin Mine on the road to Madron and Penzance, you can see some of the moorland's most interesting relics: Chun Castle, an Iron Age fort; Chun Cromlech, a chamber tomb; Lanyon Quoit; and the oldest – possibly Roman – mine, the Ding Dong. From Zennor, the Neolithic Zennor Quoit, unique in that it covers two tombs, and Giant's Rock, a logan stone on the hill above the church, are both invitingly close.

Snapshot of Mousehole.

NEWLYN ART

Back in Penzance, leave the town along the promenade. The first building on the left (in New Road) on reaching **Newlyn ⑤** is the large, light space of the **Newlyn Art Gallery** (www.newlyn artgallery.co.uk; Mon–Sat 10am–5pm, closed Mon in winter). The gallery features the work of artists of regional, national and international importance, and introduces Newlyn as the home of one of Britain's leading art colonies. Here, Stanhope Forbes, Norman Garstin, 'Lamorna' Birch and others set up easels and sent their paintings to the Royal Academy in London. But pretty little Newlyn is not all about art: it has a thriving fishing industry as well.

MOUSEHOLE AND LAMORNA

Downhill from Newlyn Bridge crossroads is **Mousehole ⑥** (pronounced *Mowzel*), the archetypal Cornish fishing village. Guests are accommodated in granite cottages in the alleys and courtyards on the hill above.

Continue along the B3315, and after about a mile, turn left at Trewoofe to run alongside a trout stream down

St Michael's Mount has a harbour but can be reached by land at low tide.

the delightful **Lamorna Valley**. A few cottages, an old mill and an inn called The Wink are the setting for a summer idyll. Granite from the quarry was shipped at **Lamorna Cove** to build London's Thames Embankment.

TO MINACK

A mile or so along the B3315 lies a Bronze Age ceremonial site, the Merry Maidens, after which the road soon leads to the village of Treen. From a car park, **Logan Rock**, a huge boulder on the crest of the spectacular headland of Treryn Dinas, can be reached by a footpath.

At nearby **Porthcurno** ❼ is a beautiful beach of golden sand, with just behind it the fascinating **Telegraph Museum** (www. telegraphmuseum.org; Apr–Oct daily 10am–5pm, Nov–Mar Sat–Mon 11am–4.30pm). The museum is partly housed in World War II fortified tunnels in the cliff.

Summer brings actors to Porthcurno and the **Minack Theatre** ❽ (www. minack.com; Apr–Sept daily 9.30am–5.30pm, Oct–Mar 10am–3.30pm; tel: 01736-810 181 for information on afternoon closures on performance days and tickets for performances). This cliff-edge amphitheatre, constructed in the 1930s, was the vision of one woman, the remarkable Rowena Cade.

Flag to show lifeguard presence.

Lanyon Quoit is thought to have been used for ritual activity.

LAND'S END

The B3315 joins the A30 for **Land's End** ❾, England's most westerly point. Nothing except the Isles of Scilly lies between here and America. The **Land's End Visitor Centre** (tel: 01736-871-501; www.landsend-landmark.co.uk; daily 10am–closing times vary; free, charge for car park and attractions) is a fun family day out in a complex that embraces a hotel, cafés, interactive and 4-D attractions, birdwatching, speciality shopping and, of course – the famous Land's End signpost.

As you leave on the Penzance road, **Sennen**, England's westernmost village, promises hospitality at the First and Last Inn. Tiny **Sennen Cove**, tucked in under the hill at the western end of Whitesand Bay surfing beach, has pretty thatched cottages and a showcase for modern crafts in the former capstan house.

ST JUST TO ZENNOR

Branching left from the Penzance road, the B3306 soon passes an airfield from which you can fly to the Isles of Scilly (see page 108), and then enters **St Just** ❿, capital of an industry that died with the fall in the

Spectacular Minack Theatre: the name means 'rocky place' in Cornish.

price of tin. With the predominance of granite and slate the town looks rather severe, but it's a friendly place. Cape Cornwall Street leads to **Cape Cornwall**, crowned with a monumental mine chimney.

The coast road traverses an area once mined intensively for tin and copper. July 2006 saw the Cornwall and West Devon Mining Landscape added to the Unesco World Heritage Site list; the Crown's Mine at **Botallack** has the most picturesque of the old mine buildings, with engine houses perched precariously on the cliff. The restored **Levant Beam En-** gine (NT; tel: 01736-786 156; mid-Mar–Oct daily 10.30am–5pm) is the oldest working beam engine in Cornwall. Half a mile (1km) along the cliff is **Geevor Tin Mine Museum** (tel: 01736-788 662; www.geevor.com; Apr–Oct Sun–Fri 9am–5pm, Nov–Mar 10am–4pm, last visit and underground tour an hour before closing).

Continuing on the B3306, a church tower signals a chapel, inn and little group of granite dwellings, set among fields strewn with enormous boulders. This is **Zennor ⓫**, where a legendary mermaid lured a chorister beneath the waves after falling in love

Cornish Souvenirs

Apart from model lighthouses and whimsical piskies (Cornish pixies), the main things to buy in Cornwall, as gifts or souvenirs, are food items – gift-wrapped boxes of fudge in an array of flavours are popular, and so is clotted cream, if it isn't going to be transported too far. Paintings, drawings or ceramic pieces are also a good choice. There are plenty of galleries and shops to choose from, especially in St Ives, Marazion and Fowey, and some of the work is of high quality.

Gifts for sweet friends.

The incomparable harbour at St Ives.

with his voice; a carving of the mermaid can be seen in St Senara church.

ST IVES

The twisting road from Zennor skirts the hills and enters **St Ives** ⑫, the most lively and interesting of all Cornwall's resorts. The road passes Higher Stennack and the **Leach Pottery**, established in 1920 by the late Bernard Leach; some of his work is exhibited here, along with that of other potters.

'The Island'

The most distinguished physical feature of St Ives is 'The Island', which

Modern art in Tate St Ives.

divides the Atlantic surfing beach of Porthmeor from the harbour and from the smaller beach of Porthminster.

Pilchards made St Ives prosperous. Houses were built with fish processing in mind, since salting and packing in barrels for export took place in the cellars below the living quarters. Local industry suffered economic disaster with the disappearance of pilchards, while the miners endured the collapse of the tin market. Survival came from an unexpected quarter: the unique quality of the light and the appeal of the subject matter began to attract artists.

The Tate

Cornwall has its own major art gallery in **Tate St Ives** (tel: 01736-796 226; www.tate.org.uk/stives; Mar–Oct daily 10am–5.20pm, Nov–Feb Tue–Sun 10am–4.20pm). It holds a permanent collection of works by St Ives painters – such as Ben Nicholson, Peter Lanyon, Patrick Heron, Sir Terry Frost and Alfred Wallis – also presenting changing displays from the main Tate Collection, with a focus on works connected with Cornwall, and temporary exhibitions of works by other artists. The building is a delight in itself, as is its position, opposite Porthmeor beach: the view is like a spectacular painting. With a new

Barbara Hepworth's garden.

In 1949 a splinter group of modern artists formed the **Penwith Society of Arts**, which exhibits at the **Penwith Gallery** (www.penwithgallery.com; Mon–Sat 10am–5pm), Back Road West. The **St Ives Museum** (www.museumsincornwall.org.uk; Apr–Oct Mon–Fri 10am–4.30pm, Sat 10am–3.30pm) covers local history.

The tall granite tower of 15th-century **St Ia** church impresses most from the sea. Inside are barrel roofs, bench-ends, carved columns and Barbara Hepworth's 1954 *Madonna and Child*.

extension cut into the cliff in 2017, twice as much art is now on display, and there are some great views from the public roof garden and restaurant.

An integral part of the Tate is the **Barbara Hepworth Museum** (same times as the Tate) in Trewyn Studio on Barnoon Hill. Hepworth's vital spirit is much in evidence in her studio and sculpture garden.

The **St Ives Society of Artists** (founded 1927) shows excellent works at a gallery housed in the light, airy nave of the old Mariners' Church (www.stisa.co.uk; Mon–Sat 10.30am–5.30pm, also Sun 2–5pm Apr–Oct), in Norway Square, behind the Sloop Inn. The **Crypt Gallery** also has special exhibitions.

CARBIS BAY AND PARADISE PARK

The A3074 climbs above St Ives' railway station, with panoramic back views over the town, and passes through Carbis Bay where a diversion left leads to the superb Carbis Bay beach.

At **Lelant**, a golf course and church share the sand-hills of the Hayle estuary. Further on, at Hayle, **Paradise Park** (www.paradisepark.org.uk; daily from 10am, last admission 5pm, 3pm winter) is the home of the World Parrot Trust, where rare birds and other creatures can be admired.

St Ives Bay Line

Arriving into St Ives by train is far easier and greener than driving, and the 14-minute journey from St Erth offers spectacular views you cannot see from the road. Opened in 1877, the St Ives Bay Line was the last railway line in Britain to be built to Brunel's broad gauge and is superbly engineered to hug the edge of the cliff around the coast. See www.gwr.com for more information.

A train creeps into St Ives.

The cliffs and beach at pretty St Agnes.

HAYLE TO GODREVY LIGHTHOUSE

East of St Ives is the heart of Cornwall's former mining industry. **Hayle** ⑬ makes an appropriate introduction because the great beam engines were made here. In **Millpond Gardens**, the foundry's ruins have been laid out as a park.

The road follows the canal through **Copperhouse**, which lost its tin and copper smelting to Swansea. Left at the crossroads beyond, the B3301 passes the *towans* (sand-hills), with splendid views of St Ives across the bay, to reach **Gwithian**.

Just out to sea is the **Godrevy Lighthouse**, the inspiration for Virginia Woolf's 1927 novel *To the Lighthouse*, and beyond is Navax Point (NT), a breeding place for seals. A road forks right from the coast and right again to regain the A30 outside Camborne.

MINES AND ENGINES

At the end of April **Camborne** ⑭ honours Richard Trevithick, 'Father of the Locomotive'. His statue outside the Library on Trevenson Street clutches a model of his steam locomotive, which anticipated Stephenson's *Rocket* by 12 years, but it was for his high-pressure steam-pumping engine that Camborne has most to thank him. There is little else to see here: Camborne is a town that lost its industry and gained few tourists.

At **Pool**, on the A3047, just outside town, **East Pool Mine** (NT; tel: 01209-315 027; mid-Mar–Oct Tue–Sat 10.30am–5pm, with exceptions) Cornish beam engines have been lovingly restored and are working smoothly. The first is visible on the right; the other, larger engine and an abandoned mine complex incorporate an audio-visual presentation tucked behind the supermarket car park to the left. Here you can find pick up leaflets about the Great Flat Lode Trail and Coast to Coast Trail, part of the **Mineral Tramways Heritage Project**, open to walkers and cyclists (www.cor

Remains of a mining past.

nish-mining.org.uk/areas-places-activities/mineral-tramways).

Continuing the mining theme, nearby Heartlands (www.heartlands-cornwall.com; daily 10am–4pm; free, charge for parking) was born out of a former mining site. Interactive exhibitions detail the rise and fall of tin mining in Cornwall, complemented by botanical gardens and an adventure playground.

REDRUTH

Continue east on the A3047 and turn right onto the A393 for **Redruth** ⓯. The Scotsman William Murdock is Redruth's revered celebrity and Murdock Day is celebrated every June. A prolific inventor, his best-known achievement is gas lighting. His house in Cross Street was the first to be lit by gas.

PORTREATH

Francis Basset, a local benefactor, created **Portreath** ⓰ – reached from Redruth by the B3300 – because there was no suitable port from which to ship ore and import Welsh coal and timber. The harbour, constructed in 1760, was superseded in the early 1800s by a more ambitious one with two inner docks. It is the starting point of the **Coast to Coast Trail**, part of the Mineral Tramways project, and cycles can be hired in Redruth and Bissoe.

ST AGNES

At Scorrier take the A30 towards Newquay, then go left on the B3277 to reach friendly little **St Agnes** ⓱. The village, the cliffs and 600ft (180m), heather-clad St Agnes Beacon all show signs of a mining past. Mining, fishing and folklore take precedence in the **St Agnes Museum** (www.stagnesmuseum.org.uk; Easter–Nov daily 10.30am–5pm; free) in Penwinnick Road, but the prize exhibit is a giant leatherback turtle, washed ashore in 1988.

Eating Out

Penzance
The Bay
Brighton Hill; tel: 01736-366 890; www.thebaypenzance.co.uk; daily 7am–9pm.
Food cooked to perfection all day and sweeping views across the bay. ££
Mousehole
Old Coastguard Inn
The Parade; tel: 01736-731 222. www.oldcoastguardhotel.co.uk; daily lunch and dinner
Praised for its seafood fresh from the boat and sea views. ££
St Ives
The Cornish Deli
3 Chapel Street; tel: 01736-795 100; www.cornishdeli.com; daily breakfast, lunch and dinner (summer only),

closed Sun in winter.
The key to everything here is local; seafood, cheese, vegetables and so much more. £
Porthminster Beach Café
Porthminster Beach; tel: 01736-795 352; www.porthminstercafe.co.uk; daily breakfast, lunch and dinner, closed dinner Sun–Wed in winter.
Chic, award-winning Mediterranean and Asian seafood restaurant. £££
St Agnes
Taste
40 Vicarage Road; tel: 01872-552 194; Tue–Sat lunch and dinner, Sun lunch.
The accolades come thick and fast for this delightful small restaurant with high quality cuisine. ££

Port Isaac, off the Atlantic Highway.

Tour 12

The North Coast Resorts and the Atlantic Highway

Holiday homes, golfers and surfers claim the coastline from Perranporth to Padstow on this 76-mile (122km) tour, while the A39 Atlantic Highway takes a step back at Newquay.

This tour explores a wonderful mix of contrasting landscapes. It could be done in a day but you will get a lot more out of a two-day trip.

PERRANPORTH

Perranporth ❶, the first stop on this northern coast, is reached along the winding B3285 from St Agnes. Surfers will find all they need here, and the great stretch of **Perran Sands** is popular with families. The B3285 joins the A3075 at Goonhavern and heads towards Newquay.

NEWQUAY

Newquay ❷ is the biggest and brashest resort on the coast and a magnet

for serious surfers. From the south, the road into town crosses the head of the Gannel estuary, and leads **to Fistral Bay**, biggest of the town's three beaches and where the major surfing championships and events are held.

Turning right towards the town centre, you must follow the one-way sys-

Surfers in Fistral Bay.

tem. Close to Fore Street is the pretty harbour, and some of the town's oldest houses poised above a sheer cliff face. A road (and a flight of steps) spirals down to the quays, where there's a sandy beach at low tide.

Family entertainment

Newquay is crammed with amusement arcades and fast-food joints, and also has a wealth of family entertainment. The **Blue Reef Aquarium** (www.bluereefaquarium.co.uk; daily from 10am, last admission 4pm, with seasonal variations) on Towan Promenade is informative and entertaining, and holds fish-feeding demonstrations. **Newquay Zoo** (tel: 01637-873 342; www.newquayzoo.org.uk; daily 10am–5pm; hours may change, call to check) at Trenance, off Edgcumbe Avenue, places emphasis on efforts to save animals through captive breeding. With close to 1,000 of the world's rarest and endangered animals the zoo is a great place for children to get up close up to a host of animals and learn more about conservation,

CHANGE OF PACE

From Newquay take the A392, and turn right on the A3058 to Kestle Mill where signs point to **Trerice ❸** (NT; tel: 01637-875 404; house: Mar–Oct daily 11am–5pm, gardens: 11am–5pm). Of all Cornwall's country houses, this glorious Elizabethan manor is the most exquisitely furnished and decorated.

A return to Kestle Mill and the fringes of Newquay leads to a drive

Railway bridge for cyclists.

along the A3059, past Newquay Cornwall Airport to **St Columb Major**. It is a peaceful village with a lovely old church and a couple of antique shops that alone would make the detour worthwhile.

THE VALE OF LANHERNE

Back on the A3059, a first right turn running through woods of the Vale of Lanherne descends to **St Mawgan** and the Falcon Inn. Beyond the wall opposite the church door is **Lanherne**, which has been the seat of the Arundell family since 1231.

COASTAL DIVERSIONS

The hill across the stream and a left-hand turn at the top follows the Vale down to **Mawgan Porth**, where evidence of a 10th-century village coexists with 21st-century holiday accommodation. Northwards, the cliff road climbs to **Bedruthan Steps ④**, rocks rising from the sand that were, according to legend, the giant Bedruthan's stepping stones. **Porthcothan**, where cliffs with caves and arches are protected by the National Trust, begins a series of beaches suitable for swimming: **Treyarnon**, **Constantine**, **Mother Ivey's Bay** and **Harlyn**, all of which are accessible from the B3276.

PADSTOW

Padstow ⑤ lies up the estuary beyond the Doom Bar, the sandbank that wrecked many a ship attempting to reach harbour in stormy conditions. The Bar and a silted-up estuary have plagued Padstow for centuries, but it still sustains a small fishing fleet and has an attractive setting.

The church sits below the grounds of **Prideaux Place** (prideauxplace. co.uk; Easter, mid-May–Oct Sun–Thu 1.30–5pm, last tour 4pm, grounds: 10.30–5pm), located to the left of the B3276 as you enter Padstow. Home of the Prideaux-Brune family, the richly furnished Elizabethan mansion has often been used as a location for films.

Down on the quay, visitors enjoy themselves admiring the harbour views and frequenting the small shops, cafés and restaurants that cater to all tastes and pockets – although Rick Stein's impact has raised the culinary tone of the town.

On North Quay, ancient **Abbey House** is believed to have been the site of a chapel. From the slipway here, beside the tourist office, the Black Tor ferry runs across the estuary to Rock (daily year-round) and water taxis run throughout the evening until midnight (Easter–Oct).

In Market Place, **Padstow Museum** (www.padstowmuseum.co.uk;

Prideaux Place is a wonderfully restored Elizabethan mansion.

Mon–Sat Apr–Sept 10.30am–4pm, Nov–Mar 11am–3pm; free) has displays on lifeboats, schooners, shipwrecks, and on the railway that came and went.

The A39 **Atlantic Highway coast** is much loved: romantics flock to Tintagel in search of King Arthur, to Morwenstow in homage to the Reverend Hawker, and to Boscastle, where Thomas Hardy found his first love.

WADEBRIDGE

From Padstow, the A389 dips to pretty **Little Petherick**, with an ancient stone bridge and church, at the head of the creek. Shortly, a right turn from the bypass descends to **Wadebridge ❻**. A steam railway, the first in Cornwall and second in England, linked Bodmin with Wadebridge in 1834, and in 1899 a branch to Padstow was opened.

The tracks have gone, but the **Camel Trail** for walkers and cy-

Padstow, one of Cornwall's most famous villages, maintains a fishing fleet and prides itself on good restaurants pioneered by Rick Stein.

clists has replaced them. Wadebridge Station now houses the **John Betjeman Centre** (tel: 01208-812 392; Mon–Fri 10am–4pm).

ROCK AND RUMPS

Rock, signposted off the A39 above the bridge, has been connected by ferry to Padstow since the 14th century. Popular with the London rich, it has been dubbed 'Chelsea-on-Sea'. Just beyond Polzeath is **Rumps**, an Iron Age hill fort on a headland.

FROM TRELIGHTS TO PORT ISAAC

Take the B3314 north from Wadebridge and at **Trelights**, en route to St Endellion and behind Long Cross Hotel, is the **Long Cross Victorian Garden** (www.longcrosshotel.co.uk; Apr–Oct daily 10am–6pm). A maze of paths makes every turn in this 2.5-acre (1-hectare) garden of shrubs and herbaceous borders a delight.

From the churchyard at St Endellion on the B3314 a twisting lane drops down to **Port Isaac ❼**. Fish cellars, an inn, a stream and closely packed cottages make it fascinating to explore.

DELABOLE

Over the headland at **Port Gaverne** schooners once loaded slate from De-

A fishing boat beached beneath the cottages at Port Isaac.

labole off the beach, and pilchards filled the fish cellars. The continuing road joins the B3314 again to enter a village that owes its existence to a hole in the ground – the biggest man-made hole in Britain. **Delabole Slate Quarry** (www.delaboleslate.co.uk/quarry-tours.asp; May–Aug Mon–Fri presentations and tours at 2pm, not BH Mon), down a short road on the right past quarrymen's cottages and chapels, has been worked since medieval times.

Just before the main junction with the A39 turn right for **Camelford ❽**. The long downhill street to the bridge over the River Camel has some attractive buildings. At the entrance to the town is the **North Cornwall Museum and Gallery** (tel: 01840-212 954; Apr–Sept Mon–Sat 10am–5pm). Country trades – those of farmer, cider-maker, carpenter, saddler, cooper, blacksmith – are well represented in re-creating life in moorland parishes over a century ago.

The first right-hand turning from the hill above the Camel bridge allows the closest approach by car to **Rough Tor** (1,312ft/400m), one of Bodmin Moor's two main heights (the other is Brown Willy). Returning to Camelford, a lane on the other side of the A39 crosses a stream at **Slaughterbridge**, the site of King Arthur's last battle and his death. The **Arthurian Centre** (www.arthur-online.co.uk; Easter–Oct daily 10am–5pm) has a 'Land of Arthur' exhibition and King Arthur's Stone.

TINTAGEL

Tintagel ❾, suffused with Arthurian legend, is hugely popular so don't go looking for mystical tranquillity. Go late in the afternoon, if you can, when the coach parties will have departed. As you enter the village, **King Arthur's Great Halls** (tel: 01840-770 526; Easter–Oct daily 10am–5pm, with exceptions) are straight in front

King Arthur's Tintagel Castle has a dramatic cliff-top setting.

of you, in Fore Street, offering a crash course in the Arthurian Experience – Arthur's story in laser lights, music and sound. The **Old Post Office** (NT; tel: 01840-770 024; Apr–Sept–Oct daily 10.30am–5.30pm, mid-Mar and Oct 11am–4pm) is a short way down the road.

  Tintagel Castle ❿ (tel: 01840-770 328; www.english-heritage.org. uk; Apr–Oct daily 10am–6pm, Oct until 5pm, Nov–Mar Sat–Sun 10am–4pm, with exceptions) is a short walk from the village. The site, accessible only by a footbridge, is set in a coastline of dramatic black and craggy cliffs, exposed to the fury of the Atlantic. The site was once occupied by Celts, Romans and Normans. In the 13th century, Henry III's brother, Richard, Earl of Cornwall, began a castle which

300 years later had become 'sore wetherbeten and yn ruin'.

SHRINE AND VALLEY

North of Tintagel, beyond Bossiney at Trethevy, the B3263 crosses a stream opposite a free car park. Follow the signs on foot down a path leading to **St Nectan's Glen**, with a 60ft (18m) waterfall and a shrine called St Nectan's Kieve (www.st-nectansglen. co.uk; daily Apr–Oct 9.30am–5pm, Nov–Mar 10.30am–3pm). Many people regard the shrine as a sacred site.

  You reach **Boscastle** ⓫ by way of Paradise, the hilltop area around the Napoleon Inn, and descend, on the right, the steep village street lined with ancient, whitewashed cottages. From the main car park a path follows the beautiful Valency Valley to the church

The Camel Trail

The Camel Trail covers just under 18 miles (28km), following the course of the old LSWR railway line, between Padstow and Blisland. Bikes can be hired from Bridge Bike Hire near the Old Bridge in Wadebridge (tel: 01208-813 050; www.bridgebikehire.co.uk). You can, of course, bring your own bike, and join the trail at various points.

The Camel Trail near Padstow.

Typical whitewashed cottage in Boscastle, now a tearoom.

of **St Juliot**, where, in 1870, young Thomas Hardy, on an architectural mission to restore the local church, met his first wife, Emma, sister-in-law of the rector. The fascinating **Museum of Witchcraft** (www.museumofwitchcraft.com; Apr–Oct Mon–Sat 10.30am–6pm, Sun 11.30am–6pm, with exceptions) showcases quirky witchcraft artefacts. In 2004 Boscastle suffered one of the worst floods in Britain's history, though no lives were lost, and buildings were restored with more flood defences put in place.

BUDE

From Boscastle, the B3263 joins the A39 for **Bude** ⑫. The river struggles through the sand to the Haven, dividing the swimmers and surfers of Summer-

leaze and Crooklets beaches, and the golfers and tennis players on the cliffs above, from the castle in the dunes and the canal on the south side. **Bude Canal**, begun in 1823 with the intention of linking the Bristol and English channels, reached no further than Launceston, and the arrival of the railway in the 1890s ended its working life. Only a short length of water remains.

Bude Canal's history is told in the **Bude** Castle **Heritage Centre** (tel: 01288-357 300; Easter–Oct daily 10am–5pm, Nov–Easter until 4pm; free), which is housed in a castle surrounded by landscaped grounds. The

Rev Hawker (1803–75), poet and the man behind Harvest Festival.

Hawker's Legacy

From 1834 to 1875, the Rev Robert Hawker was parson of St John's church in Morwenstow. An eccentric but compassionate man, he gave Christian burial to sailors from ships wrecked below the treacherous cliffs. In the churchyard is the figurehead of the *Caledonia*, the sailing ship from Arbroath in Scotland whose crew found a resting place here in 1842. Hawker also revived a pagan custom when he gave an autumn thanksgiving service in his church in 1843: Harvest Festival, as it became known, is now so much a part of church ritual that it is easy to forget that it was Hawker's creation.

small castle was built as a seaside residence in 1850 by Sir Goldsworthy Gurney, inventor of one of the earliest steam locomotives and of the Bude Light, which was used to illuminate the House of Commons.

THE VICAR OF MORWENSTOW

The A39 continues towards the Devon border. Two diversions can be made en route: first to the beautiful **Coombe Valley**; second to **Morwenstow**, Cornwall's northernmost point. This was the parish of eccentric 19th-century vicar, Robert Hawker. Near the top of the treacherous cliffs is **Hawker's Hut**, the timber-framed shack where he watched out for ships in danger, mourned his wife and sought inspiration for his poetry. It is under the protection of the National Trust and must be its smallest property.

Eating Out

Newquay
Beach Hut Bistro
Watergate Bay; tel: 01637-860 877; www.watergatebay.co.uk; daily breakfast, lunch and dinner.
This cheerful restaurant is an extremely popular place to hang out. Enjoy brilliant breakfasts, lazy lunches, sundowner drinks and great fish dishes, all with stunning views. Best to book. ££

Fifteen Cornwall
Watergate Bay; tel: 01637-861 000; www.fifteencornwall.co.uk; daily breakfast, lunch and dinner.
Jamie Oliver's beachfront, Italian-inspired venture offers excellent fresh fish and organic produce from local farmers, fishermen and growers. £££

The Boathouse
Off South Quay Hill; tel: 01637-874 062; www.the-boathouse-newquay. co.uk; daily lunch and dinner.
Innovative fish and seafood combinations with a speciality in lobster, but non-fish and vegetarian options are plentiful. ££

Mawgan Porth
Carnewas Tea Rooms
Bedruthan Steps; tel: 01637-860 701; www.carnewas-tea-rooms.co.uk; mid-Feb–Oct daily 10.30am– 5pm.
An idyllic setting for freshly-cooked

lunches, cakes and unforgettable cream teas. £

Padstow
Paul Ainsworth at No 6
6 Middle Street; tel: 01841-532 093; www.number6inpadstow.co.uk; Tue–Sat lunch and dinner, closed mid-Jan–mid-Feb
Inspiring chef Paul Ainsworth sources the best seasonal ingredients served in simple modern style, creating amazing flavours. £££

The Seafood Restaurant
Riverside; tel: 01841-532 700; www. rickstein.com; daily lunch and dinner.
This Rick Stein haven has a central seafood bar where you can watch his chefs at work (£££). For Stein bistro classics visit St Petroc's (New Street; £££) or for a less expensive Stein experience, try his café (Middle Street; ££).

Bude
Life's a Beach
Summerleaze Beach; tel: 01288-355 222; www.lifesabeach.info; daily daytime menu 10.30am–3.30pm and dinner.
Overlooking the beach and with fabulous seafood at reasonable prices. A wide-ranging menu reflects the creativity of the young talented chefs. ££.

St Mary's beach.

Tour 13

The Isles of Scilly

With such clear air, vivid blue water and year-round warmth, the Isles of Scilly seem far from Britain. Prepare to island-hop and don't be in a rush.

This small cluster of islands 28 miles (45km) southwest of Land's End comprises five inhabited islands (pop. 2,300) and over 100 smaller islands. The islands are tiny – the largest, St Mary's, is barely 3 miles (5km) at its widest point. A mild climate means tropical plants and bulbs thrive; together with tourism these form the mainstay of the economy, although the flower industry is declining. The islands can be equally magical in bad weather. In winter they face the full force of the Atlantic. For details of how to get here, see page 121.

MYTH AND REALITY

Steeped in myth and legend, the islands have been associated with the Arthurian Lyonesse, the Atlantis of

> **Highlights**
>
> - Isles of Scilly Museum
> - Tresco Abbey Gardens
> - Bryher
> - St Agnes
> - St Martin's

the Greeks and the Cassiterides (tin islands) of the Phoenicians. What is certain is that they have been inhabited for at least 4,000 years, as countless Bronze Age burial mounds testify.

For much of their history, the islanders had to scratch a living from anything the sea had to offer, including shipwrecks. Prosperity only arrived in 1834 when Augustus Smith obtained the lease of the islands. He

World Pilot Gig Championship, Hugh Town.

made social reforms and encouraged shipbuilding.

ST MARY'S

Shipyards once occupied the beach adjacent to the quayside at **St Mary's**, the first port of call for visitors arriving by sea. It is only a short walk into the Scillies' main town, **Hugh Town**, which straddles the island at its narrowest point. You could visit the **Mermaid** pub before continuing up the road on the right, through the **Garrison Gate** to **Star Castle**. Now a hotel, the castle was built in 1593 as protection against pirates and possible invasion by the Spanish. In 1646, during the Civil War, the castle was a refuge for the Prince of Wales (Charles II) and his retinue after their defeat at Bodmin.

ISLES OF SCILLY MUSEUM

Continue through Hugh Town into Church Street, where the **Isles of Scilly Museum** ❶ (www.iosmuseum.org; Mon–Sat, Easter–Sept 10am–4.30pm, Sat until noon, Oct–Easter 10am–noon) offers an interesting insight into life on the islands. Exhibits range from Bronze and Iron Age artefacts to remnants of shipwrecks. The museum's centrepiece is a restored pilot boat (gig). A natural history section highlights species that live here for at least part of the year. The puffin and the Atlantic seal are popular residents of the Western Rocks.

St Mary's has some magnificent coastline, nowhere more than at **Penninis Head** on the south coast. There is also much evidence of ancient history on the island, including **Bant's Carn Burial Chamber**.

Tresco is dotted with almost deserted white-sand beaches.

TRESCO

Depending on the tide, visitors to the paradise island of **Tresco** usually arrive at **New Grimsby** harbour. A long promenade leads around the harbour, where the road turns left up-hill to Old Grimsby. Most visitors continue straight on, following signs to **Tresco Abbey Gardens** ❷ (www. tresco.co.uk/enjoying/abbey-garden; daily 10am–4pm, café closed Nov–Mar). Laid out in the 19th century by Augustus Smith, the gardens contain rare plants from 80 countries, rang-

ing from Brazil to New Zealand and Burma to South Africa, many brought back by ships' captains. In the gardens is the **Valhalla Museum**, devoted to figureheads culled from shipwrecks.

The southern end of Tresco is flanked by a series of beautiful, empty beaches. Continue along the east coast past Pentle Bay and the Old Blockhouse to **Old Grimsby**, from where it is possible to explore the rugged northern end of the island, whose features include **Pipers' Hole**, a cave with a small underground lake. On the west coast the most distinctive man-made feature is the tower of **Cromwell's Castle**, built on the promontory beneath the older King Charles' Castle in 1651.

Cromwell's Castle on Tresco, built beneath King Charles' Castle.

BRYHER

Just opposite Tresco is **Bryher** ❸, the smallest of the five inhabited islands, with a population of around 80. The settled part of the island starts at the **church** by the main quay and winds uphill, dropping down to the coast once more at the **Fraggle Rock Café** (see page 111). A path leads up to the northern tip, offering beautiful walks over the downs. The rocky headland of **Shipman Head**

The most beautiful feature at the island's southern end, **Rushy Bay** overlooks uninhabited **Samson** island. Behind the bay is **Samson Hill**, from which there are superb views.

ST AGNES AND ST MARTIN'S

St Agnes ❹ is the most southwesterly community in the whole of the British Isles. Principal industries are fishing and flower growing. At low tide you can walk across a sandbar to the small island of **Gugh**. Near the main jetty is the Turk's Head, renowned for good food and fine views. In the centre of the island, and visible from afar, is a disused, 17th-century, coal-burning lighthouse. An even more striking feature, the red-and-white-striped Daymark dominates the easternmost inhabited island of **St Martin's ❺**, popular for its magnificent beaches.

is separated from the island by a narrow cleft; so having visited **Hell Bay**, which even on a day of moderate swell offers spectacular views of the sea lashing against the rocks, walkers can continue down the west coast.

Eating Out

St Mary's
Bell Rock Hotel Restaurant
Church Street; tel: 01720-422 575; www.bellrockhotel.co.uk; daily dinner only.
This cosy restaurant uses local produce whenever possible such as sea trout, prawns and Cornish cheeses. ££

Juliet's Garden
Seaways Flower Farm, Portloo Beach; tel: 01720-422 228; www.julietsgardenrestaurant.co.uk; Apr–Oct daily lunch and dinner.
Views from the terrace over the harbour are breathtaking and the food is extraordinary (especially Juliet's signature dish – lobster and crab omelette). A converted barn loft provides the indoor seating. ££.

Strudel in Town
Thorofare, Hugh Town; tel: 01720-422

440; www.strudelonscilly.com; daily 9.30am–4.30pm
You get great views from this café, which serves unlikely Bavarian lunches and first-class coffee. £

Bryher
Fraggle Rock Bar
tel: 01720-422 222; daily lunch and dinner, reduced hours in winter.
England's most westerly pub, the Fraggle Rock provides drinks, snacks (including the famous crab double-decker sandwich) and evening meals. £

St Martin's
Seven Stones Inn
Lower Town; tel: 01720-423 777; daily lunch and dinner, closed Mon–Tue, Thu in winter
Family-run inn taking pride in serving a good pint and exceptional pub grub, which arguably has the best pub view in the world. ££

Surfers at Fistral Bay,
Newquay.

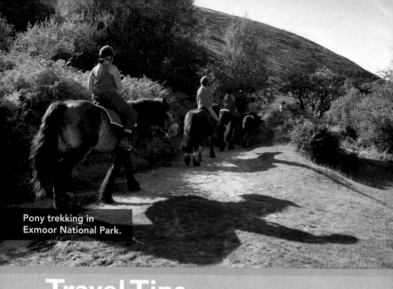

Pony trekking in
Exmoor National Park.

Travel Tips

Active Pursuits

The great outdoors of Devon and Cornwall are ideal for all kinds of outdoor activities. Choose from walking, cycling, golf, riding, fishing and all manner of water sports, including, of course, surfing.

WALKING

Devon's most famous **long-distance routes** are the Templer Way, Two Moors Way, Tarka Trail, and the South West Coast Path. Both moors have guided walks, organised by the National Parks themselves and usually with a ranger as guide. Check out www.visitdevon.co.uk or www.exploredevon.info for detailed information.

In Cornwall the South West Coast Path, the Camel Trail and Cardinham Woods all offer great walking. Also worth it if you are in Cornwall in the autumn is the South East Cornwall Walking Festival (see www.visitcornwall.com for information) with a se-ries of walks to enjoy throughout the area. Themes include wildlife, history and heritage, storytelling, conservation and geology. For information on the South West Path, visit www.southwestcoastpath.org.uk. For information on the 'Right to Roam' legislation check www.ramblers.org.uk. Other useful sites include www.nationaltrust.org.uk/lists/walking-in-cornwall and www.cornwallwildlifetrust.org.uk.

CYCLING

Some walks have also been designated **cycleways**, but mountain bikers are asked to stick to the agreed routes. Bikes can be hired throughout the counties. For useful information on the major routes and details of cycle hire opportunities, check out www.visitdevon.co.uk; https://new.devon.gov.uk/cycling and www.visitcornwall.com.

Cornish Cycle Tours (www.cornishcycletours.co.uk) offers cycling holidays in Cornwall's most scenic areas, staying at charming places. For the Camel Trail, call Bridge Bike Hire, tel: 01208-813 050; www.bridgebikehire.co.uk; or Padstow Cycle Hire, tel: 01841-533 533; www.padstowcyclehire.com. For general information, check www.sustrans.org.uk/ncn/map/national-cycle-network.

Cycling in Dartmoor National Park.

FISHING

In Devon **game fishing** for trout is popular on the fringes of both moors. Local hotels usually have fishing rights, or can make arrangements for guests. The Exe, the Torridge, the Taw, the Tamar and the Dart are salmon rivers. Local hotels such as the Rising Sun at Umberleigh are popular with salmon fishermen. **Sea-fishing** in the region can be fruitful, but less so from the shore than from a boat. For general information about fishing in the South West see www.gethooked.co.uk.

GOLF

Golf links are often set in superb coastal sites. In Devon alone there are over fifty courses, including Torquay, Dartmouth, Okehampton and Ilfracombe. In Cornwall

St Enodoc Golf Club, Rock (tel: 01208-863 216; www.st-enodoc.co.uk), has two courses, as does St Mellion International Resort, Saltash (tel: 01579-351 351; www.st-mellion.co.uk), where one is designed by Jack Nicklaus. For more details, visit: www.golfindevon.co.uk and www.golfincornwall.co.uk.

HORSE RIDING

Horse riding is popular on both moors in Devon. On Exmoor try Burrowhayes Farm (tel: 01643-862 463; www.burrowhayes.co.uk) or Exmoor Riding (tel: 01643-862 816;

The Isles of Scilly teem with birdlife, such as oystercatchers.

Birdwatching

The Fal Estuary, Gerrans Bay and the surrounding coastline are ideal spots for birdwatching. A huge number of sea birds, divers, waders and sea ducks are either resident here or regular winter visitors. Most of this coastline is managed by the National Trust and there are footpaths along much of its length. For more details, contact the **Cornwall Bird Watching and Preservation Society** (www.cbwps.org.uk) or the **Cornwall Wildlife Trust** (tel: 01872-273 939; www.cornwallwildlifetrust.org.uk). Also check out www.scilly-birding.co.uk.

Family Fun Activities

The Manor House and Ashbury hotels (www.manorhousehotel. co.uk) near Okehampton are a home from home with the bonus of family fun activities. Kids can enjoy three indoor swimming pools, one with waterslides, tennis and badminton, ice and roller skating, pedal karts, indoor adventure playhouse, 'Gamezone', and lots more. With golf and craft lessons also on the menu, there's plenty for grownups too.

www.exmoor-riding.co.uk. On Dartmoor try Cholwell (tel: 01822-810 526; www.cholwellridingstables. co.uk). In Cornwall, establishments offering riding and trekking for all ages and abilities include: Polmartin Riding, (tel: 01503-220 428; www. polmartinfarm.com), Penhalwyn Trekking Centre and School, (tel: 01736-796 461; www.penhalwyn stables.co.uk) and Trenance Riding Stables, (tel: 01637-872 699; www. newquayridingstables.co.uk).

WATER SPORTS

There is excellent **white-water canoeing** on the River Dart, and to a lesser extent the Barle and the Exe in Devon. A couple of the river estuaries – notably the Dart and the creek at Salcombe – have **summer canoeing**. To hire kayaks try CRS Adventures, Ashburton, tel: 01364-653 444; www.crs adventures.com, no experience necessary. **Sea-canoeing** takes place along the south coast at Dartmouth and Salcombe, where craft can be hired.

Sailing thrives in the creeks of South Devon, particularly around Salcombe. Here Salcombe Dinghy Sailing (tel: 07809-556 457; www.salcombedin ghysailing.co.uk) organises learn-to-sail courses and also have dinghies for hire. In Cornwall the Fal and Camel estuaries offer some fine sailing. Details from sailing clubs at Falmouth (tel: 01326-211 311), Fowey (tel: 01726-833 573), Flushing (tel: 01326-374 043), Helford River (tel: 01326-231 460), Looe (tel: 01503-262 559), or the Sailing Centre, Isles of Scilly (tel: 01720-422 060). South West Lakes Trust also runs water-sports centres: www.swlakestrust.org.uk.

Sailing is a great way to explore craggy coves and inlets.

Surfers racing to the waves at Woolacombe beach.

Surfing

Cornwall's exhilarating Atlantic coast offers some of the best surfing in the country at Fistral Bay, Lusty Glaze and Watergate Bay, Newquay, and Porthmeor Beach, St Ives; but Bude, St Agnes and Perranporth are also strong contenders. In all these places you can hire or buy equipment, take lessons, and be assured of qualified instructors and lifeguards. All the schools listed below have the British Surfing Association seal of approval.

In Newquay, the West Country Surf School (Watergate Bay, tel: 07772-251 778; www.surfingschool. co.uk) offers tuition in groups, as a family or one on one, with all-in prices for lessons and equipment. Also in Newquay, at the Escape Surf School (35 Fore Street, tel: 07810-805 624; www.escapesurfschool. co.uk) lessons can be spread over six days and accommodation arranged if required. Many shops in town hire or sell equipment.

In St Ives, the St Ives Surf School (tel: 01736-793 938; www.stivessurf school.com) offers tuition and equipment hire, as does Surf's Up Surf School (tel: 01208-862 003; www. surfsupsurfschool.com) at Polzeath nearer Wadebridge. In Widemouth Bay, Bude, the environmentally aware Outdoor Adventure Multi-Activity (tel: 01288-362 900, www.outdoor adventure.co.uk) specialises in kayaking and canoeing as well as surfing, and offers accommodation. In Perranporth, the Surf School (tel: 07974-550 823; www.perranporth surfschool.co.uk) gives lessons.

For up-to-the-minute tide and wind conditions and the best surfing spots, check www.magicseaweed.com. For general surfing information, check www.cornwalls.co.uk/surfing or www. surfing-cornwall.com.

Canoes and kayaks are readily available to rent at most coastal resorts and popular beaches.

Themed Holidays

A growing interest in specialist holidays has led to several organisations offering breaks with a theme. Choose from painting, conservation work, yoga, interior design, foraging and cooking, spa sessions and more.

VOLUNTEERING

If you care passionately about the conservation of Devon and Cornwall's historic houses, gardens, coast and countryside, the National Trust offer working holidays for volunteers. Jobs include welcoming visitors, stewarding, gardening, environmental and artefact conservation. Help is needed too for the day-to-day running of buildings and open spaces, in offices and with special events.

Groundwork Devon and Cornwall also offers volunteering opportunities arranged so that participants can work different days of the week and weekends too. And Responsible Travel offers short breaks in Cornwall assisting with coastal conservation.

CONSERVATION

If you opt for a Helpful Holidays cottage break you can relax and enjoy your holiday knowing that they operate a Green Cottages scheme, which encourages their homeowners to work sustainably. At Kingsmill Farm Cottage in the Tamar Valley, Valerie Taplin has created a wildflower meadow and established a large freshwater lake.

'The cottage is on the banks of the tidal creek,' reveals Valerie, 'so guests can spot buzzards, owls, ducks, herons, swans, little egret, kingfishers, badgers and deer.'

PAINTING

If painting is your thing, consider Cornwall Painting Holidays in Newlyn. Experienced tutor Tim Hall supervises courses to help budding artists tackle a new medium, improve their skills or try painting outside. All materials are provided and class sizes are restricted, and artist in residence Henrietta Graham is available for tea and talk about painting matters. Enquire about local accommodation when booking.

Still on an artistic theme, be inspired in a fabulous setting by the St Ives School of Painting at Porthmeor Studio where classes have been run since 1938. Expert teaching

Volunteers repairing a dry-stone wall on a National Trust Working Holiday on Exmoor, Devon.

The stunning scenery begs to be immortalised on canvas.

from practising artists can be found in a range of genres and for all levels from beginners up. Or try the idyllic Brambles Art Retreat at Lifton in Devon where you can paint or draw in beautiful surroundings for a weekend or on a five- or seven-day course. The small classes ensure personal tuition in media such as watercolour, acrylic and oils.

FORAGING AND COOKING

Do you know your wood sorrel from your Cornish round leaf mint, or how about wild borage from pennywort? Foraging for wild food is the complete antithesis to supermarket homogeneity and uses new skills to find seasonal, nutritionally rich and interesting ingredients for free. It is a totally immersive experience exploring field, woodland, river and coast. As the seasons change so too does the wealth and availability of edible wild plants.

Foraging is becoming increasingly popular and there are a variety of courses to be found in both Devon and Cornwall. Caroline Davey of the wild food company, Fat Hen, is based in St Buryan near Penzance and has been running foraging and cookery courses since 2007. With a passion for nature and the environment and experience acquired from around the world, she has devised a superb variety of courses from just foraging to foraging and cooking, as well as cookery courses based around wild produce. Courses are half day, full day, weekend or bespoke, with accommodation on site (minimum one week) or in the local area. The courses range from gourmet wild food weekends and game cookery to wild vegan cookery. Expert chefs from Devon and Cornwall bring their skills to aid creations from your foraged produce, inspiring the likes of crispy laver seaweed, wild herb polenta or sea buckthorn sorbet.

YOGA AND SPA HOLIDAYS

Yoga holidays, spa breaks and meditation holidays can be booked at several venues around Cornwall. Classes are led by a qualified British Wheel of Yoga teacher and in many cases packages include spa treatments. Choose from sites at Helford River, Mawgan Porth, Newquay and Polzeath. If you are a spa aficionado, top places include St Moritz Hotel in Polzeath, located above Daymer bay in Trebetherick, and the Fistral Beach Hotel and Spa in Newquay. The Budock Vean Hotel spa on the Helford River has a heated indoor pool, log fires and over 60 acres (24 hectares) of parkland along with all the pampering you can handle.

For Elemis massage treatments, check out Newquay's Retallack Resort and Spa at St Columb. And at Falmouth's St Michael's Spa Hotel fitness fans can pump iron at a well-equipped fitness suite, try a body wrap, steam

Some Tourist Information Centres organise volunteering programmes.

chamber mud experience, swim, indulge in a massage and facial or enjoy the hydrotherapy pool.

ADVENTURE SPORTS

If you fancy getting your adrenalin going try Outdoor Adventure at Widemouth Bay, Bude which offers action-packed family holidays that include accommodation, all meals,

Devon offers excellent surfing holidays.

instruction and equipment. Choose from daredevil coasteering, surfing, bodyboarding, climbing, abseiling and much more, all undertaken in spectacular locations.

Surfing is generally associated with Cornwall, in particular Newquay, and many companies run day and longer courses. Devon, too, provides some excellent surfing beaches, with a variety of courses run from Croyde Beach by Surf South West.

USEFUL WEBSITES

www.nationaltrust.org.uk
www.groundwork.org.uk
www.responsibletravel.com
www.helpfulholidays.co.uk
www.kingsmillcornwall.co.uk
www.cornwallpaintingholidays.co.uk
www.schoolofpainting.co.uk
www.bramblesartretreat.com
www.foragers-association.org.uk
www.fathen.org
www.stmoritzhotel.co.uk
www.fistralbeachhotel.co.uk
www.budockvean.co.uk
www.retallackresort.co.uk
www.stmichaelshotel.co.uk
www.outdooradventure.co.uk
www.surfsouthwest.com

Practical Information

GETTING THERE

Devon and Cornwall are large counties with few major arteries. Public transport is widespread, but so is the population, so don't expect to get anywhere in a hurry. Schedules tend to vary according to local market days and to seasons.

By road

Most car travellers arrive in Devon via the M5 motorway, which is fed by the M4 from London (roughly 200 miles/320km) and the M6 from the north.

The nearest motorway to Cornwall, the M5 (connections with the M4 at Bristol and the M6, at Birmingham), ends at Exeter, from where the main routes into Cornwall are the A30 to Penzance and the A38 to Bodmin via Plymouth. North Cornwall is served by the Atlantic Highway (A39).

City-centre parking in Devon and Cornwall is quite good, with several multi-storey car parks. Most other locations have pay-and-display car parks, not cheap. Parking is often a problem in summer. There are a number of Park and Ride schemes, including at Lelant Saltings (for St Ives), Padstow, Falmouth, Truro and Exeter.

By coach

National Express has regular services into the region. The journey time London–Penzance is about 8.5 hours. For further information: www.nationalexpress.com or tel: 0871-781 8181.

By train

Exeter is served by fast trains (less than 3 hours) from Paddington. An alternative London slower service runs from Waterloo.

Fast trains, operated by Great Western Railway, run from London Paddington to various towns in the West. Direct journey time London–Penzance is about 6 hours; www.gwr.com. Virgin Trains run from central and northern England plus Scotland; www.virgintrains.co.uk.

For all train information, contact National Rail Enquiries, tel: 0345-748 4950; www.nationalrail.co.uk or visit www.thetrainline.com.

By air

Exeter and Newquay have airports

Exeter airport information, tel: 01392-367 433; www.exeter-airport.co.uk; Newquay Airport tel: 01637-860 600; www.newquaycornwallairport.com.

To the Isles of Scilly

There are regular flights to the Isles of Scilly with Skybus from Exeter (Mar–Oct only), Newquay and Land's End. For something more thrilling, arrive

If you are driving on the more remote roads of both counties, look out for grazing livestock!

by helicopter with Island Helicopters, which operates year-round. The Isles of Scilly Steamship Group offers fixed-wing flights and boat services, tel: 0845-710 5555; www.chycor.co.uk/tourism/issc/steamship.htm. Book air and ferry services online at www.islesofscilly-travel.co.uk.

Getting Around

By car

Many of the country lanes have narrow stretches and there are plenty of steep hills. Allow extra time for all car journeys, and don't try to hurry. The region's roads were not built for speed, and there's likely to be a tractor, herd of cows, or caravan somewhere just ahead.

In general, it is always good to know the market days of your local town, because these greatly affect the amount of traffic making its way to the centre. To steer clear of local traffic congestion, tune into BBC Radio Devon or Cornwall for regular bulletins on traffic.

Car rental

Major companies have offices in Exeter, Plymouth and Newquay.

Budget Exeter, tel: 01392-422 095
Avis Plymouth, tel: 0344-544 6090
Thrifty Plymouth, tel: 01752-207 207
Europcar Newquay, tel: 0371-384 5973

By train

From Exeter (St Davids) regional connections go to Barnstaple and Exmouth, and from Newton Abbot to Paignton. From Plymouth, a service runs up the Tamar Valley all the way to Gunnislake.

Great Western Railway operates a service between Plymouth and Penzance via Liskeard and Truro, with lines heading off to Gunnislake, Looe,

Newquay, Falmouth and St Ives. For more information on how to get around by trains visit www.greatscenicrailways.co.uk.

By bus

The local bus network is extensive and services are fairly reliable. First Cornwall (www.firstgroup.com) are the main operators throughout Cornwall and Stagecoach South West (tel: 01392-427 711; www.stagecoachbus.com) are the largest in Devon. Other services are run by Plymouth City Bus (01752-662 271; www.plymouthbus.co.uk).

By bike

Cyclists can travel several car-free routes including the Tarka Trail and Cornwall's Clay Trail. The Exe Estuary Trail is a cycling route and walkway around the entire estuary and Drake's Trail can be found between Tavistock and Plymouth.

By taxi

For short distances around cities, taxis are inexpensive.

Country lanes in Devon and Cornwall can be extremely narrow.

Train rides can be eventful along the coast.

Exe Cars, Exeter, tel: 01392-217 000, www.exetercars.com.
Need-A-Cab, Plymouth, tel: 01752-666 222, www.needacab247.com.
A2B Taxis, Newquay, tel: 01637-877 777, www.a2bnewquay.com.
Penzance Taxis, Penzance, tel: 01736-366 366, www.penzancetaxis.co.uk.

GREEN TRANSPORT

For low-impact travel use public transport. First Kernow and Stagecoach uses Drive Green technology on its buses. In August 2018 greener bi-mode trains (running on both diesel and electricity) on the London–Penzance line were introduced.

FACTS FOR THE VISITOR

Disabled travellers

For general information and accommodation visit www.goodaccessguide.co.uk.

Other useful sites to visit include: www.disabledholidaydirectory.co.uk; www.accessiblecountryside.org.uk; www.disabledaccessholidays.com; www.tourismforall.org.uk.

Emergencies

For emergency ambulance, fire or police dial 999. Accident and Emergency (A&E) Departments can be found at the following: North Devon Hospital, Raleigh Park, Barnstaple, tel: 01271-322 577; Royal Devon and Exeter Hospital, Barrack Road, Exeter, tel: 01392-411 611; Derriford Hospital, Crownhill, Plymouth, tel: 01752-202 082; The Royal Cornwall Hospital, Treliske, Truro, tel: 01872-250 000.

Opening hours

Most shops open from 9am to 5.30pm; supermarkets usually stay open later, and some open on Sunday. Post offices generally open Monday–Friday 9am to 5.30pm, and usually until noon on Saturday. There are plenty of late-night garages.

Tourist information

For information on Devon check out www.visitdevon.co.uk. For Tor Bay (Torquay, Paignton and Brixham), www.englishriviera.co.uk and for North Devon and Exmoor, www.northdevon.com. For Lundy Island, www.landmarktrust.org.uk/Lundyisland.

For information on Cornwall, check www.visitcornwall.com. For Scilly, www.visitislesofscilly.com.

Accommodation

Devon and Cornwall offer just about every type of accommodation to suit your needs and pocket. Booking is essential during high summer, but not always at other times.

Farm stays are popular, as are self-catering cottages. Holiday camps, caravan sites and camping facilities are widespread, particularly in coastal areas. To tipi or not to tipi is the perennial camping question. Tipis usually come kitted out with bed rugs, rolls, lanterns and mini cooker so you can camp in total comfort. Glamping in yurts is increasingly popular.

B&B, CAMPING AND CARAVANNING WITH THE NATIONAL TRUST

More than 80 tenants of National Trust (www.nationaltrust.org.uk) properties offer bed-and-breakfast accommodation. Most of it is fairly inexpensive and invariably the properties are attractive ones, set in rural areas. Sleeping in the great outdoors can be lots of fun too. The NT campsite at Highertown Farm has fine views of the southeast Cornwall coast and is situated near a secluded beach. If you prefer camping within walls, stay in a NT stone hut: Peppercombe Bothy on the coast at Bideford offers the simple life with incredible sea views.

There are several YHA youth hostels in the region, including on Dartmoor and Exmoor, and at Exeter, Ilfracombe, Seaton, the Lizard, Penzance and Boscastle. Camping barns, or 'stone tents', are owned by individual farmers, but co-ordinated by the YHA. Barns vary, but showers and cooking facilities are standard. Many are located on long-distance footpaths and cycle trails.

HOTELS

Price categories are for a double room with breakfast in mid-summer:
£££ = over £200
££ = £120–£200
£ = under £120

Babbacombe
Cary Arms & Spa
Beach Road; tel: 01803-327 110; www.caryarms.co.uk.
In a stunning spot on the beach, the sea-facing bedrooms and cottages capture contemporary charm with echoes of New England and have huge, comfy beds. Good gastro-pub dining and a friendly atmosphere. £££

Bigbury on Sea
Burgh Island
Tel: 01548-810 514; www.burghisland.com.
Unusual Art Deco hotel on an island first inhabited by monks in the 10th century, with access by sea tractor. Agatha Christie wrote two books while staying here. The smart clientele dress up for dinner dances. £££

Combe Martin
Sandy Cove Hotel
Old Coast Road; tel: 01271-882 243; www.sandycove-hotel.co.uk.
Expect unpretentious style and warmth at this family hotel with a spectacular outlook over the bay. The amazing swimming pool has bi-fold doors that let the outside in. ££

Dartmouth
Royal Castle Hotel
The Quay; tel: 01803-833 033; www.royalcastle.co.uk.
This former 17th-century coaching inn on the quay is a focus of the town's social scene, with lively bars,

great ambience and a respected restaurant. ££

Plymouth
Duke of Cornwall
Millbay Road; tel: 01752-275 850; www.bestwestern.co.uk/hotels/best-western-duke-of-cornwall-hotel. A true Plymouth landmark, Victorian Gothic architecture sets the tone for the character that follows inside. A stone's throw from the historic Hoe, this represents very pleasant, value-for-money accommodation. £

Ilfracombe
Epchris House
Torrs Park; tel: 01271-862 751; www.epchrisguesthouse.co.uk.
The oldest building in the Torrs, dating back to 1831, Epchris House is set in extensive secluded gardens with an outdoor heated swimming pool. The spacious bedrooms are all decorated to a high standard. ££

Marine Court
Hillsborough Road; tel: 01271-862 920; www.marinecourthoteldevon.co.uk.
In a quiet spot a short walk from the harbour, this husband and wife team

Sumptuous room at the Carlyon Bay Hotel, perched high above St Austell Bay.

extend warm hospitality at their adults-only well-appointed guest house. Some of the bedrooms have fabulous sea views and there is a pretty terrace. ££

Bolventor
Jamaica Inn
Nr Launceston; tel: 01566-86250; www.jamaicainn.co.uk.
The famous inn in a dramatic setting on the Bodmin Moor has been expanded but retains its snug, cosy atmosphere – and its ghost. It also boasts a Smugglers Museum. £

Fowey
Old Quay House Hotel
28 Fore Street; tel: 01726-833 302; www.theoldquayhouse.com.
A lovingly-restored boutique hotel in Victorian seaman's refuge. The terrace is the perfect place for pre-dinner drinks and to soak up the wonderful estuary views. ££

Newquay
Headland Hotel & Spa
Tel: 01637-872 211; www.headlandhotel.co.uk.
Grand, imposing appearance but with a family-friendly atmosphere. The hotel has a spa and is set in 10 acres (4 hectares) above Fistral Beach. 96 rooms as well as 30 self-catering cottages. ££

Penzance
Hotel Penzance
Britons Hill; tel: 01736-363 117; www.hotelpenzance.com
Perched on a hill with far-reaching views over the waterfront and harbour, this cosy townhouse hotel was converted from two Edwardian merchants' houses. A sunny terrace overlooks the Mediterranean-style garden with pool and there is an excellent restaurant. ££

Tintagel is a beautiful place to stay.

St Austell
Carlyon Bay Hotel
Sea Road; tel: 01726-812 304; www.carlyonbay.com
Luxurious 1930s hotel set in 250 acres (100 hectares) of expansive subtropical gardens, with leisure facilities including golf. £££

St Ives
Garrack Hotel
Burthallan Lane; tel: 01736-796 199; www.garrack.com.
Set on a hill near the Tate, this family-run hotel has a large garden offering great views over Porthmeor Beach. There's an indoor spa pool, a sauna and an award-winning restaurant. Private on-site parking is available. ££

Primrose House
Primrose Valley; tel: 01736-794 939; www.primroseonline.co.uk.
This delightful Edwardian villa has been given a stylish, contemporary makeover. Each room features hanging artwork and bespoke pieces, and many benefit from views of the ocean. £££

Tintagel
Bossiney House Hotel
Tel: 01840-770 240; www.bossineyhouse.com.
In a great location on the coast, this family-run hotel is far from the madding crowd (0.5 miles/1km from the village) and offers superb views, a good restaurant and family rooms. ££

Isles of Scilly
Bell Rock Hotel
Church Street, St Mary's; tel: 01720-422 575; www.bellrockhotel.co.uk.
Small, reasonably priced hotel and a great base for exploring the islands. Individual bedrooms are scattered over four floors; those on the higher floors have sea views. Indoor swimming pool. £

USEFUL WEBSITES
www.visitdevon.co.uk
www.visitcornwall.com
www.visitislesofscilly.com
www.nationaltrust.org.uk
www.airbnb.co.uk
www.coastandcountry.co.uk
www.toadhallcottages.co.uk
www.holidaycottages.co.uk
www.forestholidays.co.uk
www.laterooms.com
www.cornishfarmholidays.co.uk
www.yha.org.uk
www.devonholidays.org
www.organicholidays.co.uk
www.canopyandstars.co.uk
www.cornishtipiholidays.co.uk
www.smoothhound.co.uk
www.uniquehomestays.com

Index

Credits

Insight Guides Great Breaks Devon and Cornwall
Editor: Tatiana Wilde
Author: Jackie Staddon and Hilary Weston
Head of DTP and Pre-Press: Rebeka Davies
Managing Editor: Carine Tracanelli
Picture Editor: Tom Smyth
Cartography Update: Carte
Photo credits: Alamy 51T, 51B, 109; Apa
Publications 12, 76T; Carlyon Bay Hotel 125; Corrie
Wingate/Apa Publications 54, 62T; Danny Pyne
82B; David Bleasdale 95B; Fotolia 7M, 25, 57, 74B,
75B, 105B, 108; FremantleMedia Ltd/Rex Feature
36TL; Getty Images 8/9, 46, 59B, 61; Hoxtonboy
30T; iStock 1, 6ML, 6ML, 7BR, 14, 15, 20T, 21B,
24B, 31B, 32T, 34T, 48B, 49T, 58B, 60T, 60B, 62B,
63, 74T, 92T, 94T, 96T, 115B, 123; Lydia Evans/Apa
Publications 4/5, 6MC, 6MC, 7T, 7TR, 7MR, 9, 10,
11, 13, 16, 17, 18, 19, 21T, 22, 23, 24T, 27, 28, 29,
30B, 31T, 32B, 33, 34B, 35, 42, 43T, 43B, 44T, 44B,
45, 64, 65, 66, 67, 68, 69, 71, 73T, 73B, 75T, 76B,
77, 78TL, 78ML, 80, 82T, 84B, 85, 87T, 86B, 88T,
88B, 89, 90, 91, 92B, 93T, 93B, 94B, 95T, 96B, 97T,
98B, 98T, 100, 101, 103T, 103B, 104, 105T, 106T,
113, 114, 117B, 120B, 126; Matt Wharton 84T; Max
Hughes 102; Neil Fawcett/fotoLibra 7M; NTPL/
Andrew Butler 83; NTPL/Mark Bolton 58T; NTPL/
Stuart Cox 118; Occombe Farm 26; Public domain
36ML, 81, 106B; Rachel Lambert 87; Ronald Grant
Archive 36/37T; Scilly Isles TB 111T, 110B, 116;
Scott Zona 70; Shutterstock 20B, 49B, 72; Stuart
Berry 55; Tamsyn Williams 79T; Tim Hall 59T, 119;
Tom Page 97B; Tom Smyth 38, 39, 40, 41, 48T, 50T,
50B, 52T, 53, 56B, 56T, 115T, 117T, 120T, 121, 122;
UK Country House Hotels 52B
Cover credits: AWL Images (main)
Shutterstock (BL) iStock (BR)
No part of this book may be reproduced,
stored in a retrieval system or transmitted in
any form or means electronic, mechanical,
photocopying, recording or otherwise, without
prior written permission from Apa Publications.

CONTACT US:
Every effort has been made to provide
accurate information in this publication,
but changes are inevitable. The publisher
cannot be responsible for any resulting loss,
inconvenience or injury. We would appreciate
it if readers would call our attention to any
errors or outdated information. We also
welcome your suggestions; please contact us
at: hello@insightguides.com

All Rights Reserved
© 2019 Apa Digital (CH) AG and
Apa Publications (UK) Ltd

Fourth Edition 2019

Printed in China by CTPS
Contains Land-Form Panorama Contours
& Meridian 2 and OS Street View data
© Crown copyright and database right.

Distribution
UK, Ireland and Europe: Apa Publications
(UK) Ltd; sales@insightguides.com
United States and Canada: Ingram Publisher
Services; ips@ingramcontent.com
Australia and New Zealand: Woodslane;
info@woodslane.com.au
Southeast Asia: Apa Publications (SN) Pte;
singaporeoffice@insightguides.com
Worldwide: Apa Publications (UK) Ltd;
sales@insightguides.com
**Special Sales, Content Licensing and
CoPublishing**
Insight Guides can be purchased in bulk
quantities at discounted prices. We can
create special editions, personalised
jackets and corporate imprints tailored
to your needs. sales@insightguides.com;
www.insightguides.biz